What others are saying about "The Power of Subconscious Goal Setting"

" ... an absolutely perfect formula to connect your goals with the subconscious mind... "

- John Kanary
President, The Life Success Coach Inc.
Author of International Best Seller
Breaking Through Limitations

"Scott's knowledge of the subconscious and how it relates to the achievement of your goals shows through on every page."

- Mark Victor Hansen
Co-creator, #1 New York Times Best-Selling series
Chicken Soup for the Soul ®
Co-author, *The One Minute Millionaire*

"Scott has the ability to turn your dreams into reality. As both a colleague and a friend, I have found his vision and insight inspirational."

- Dr John Gora PhD
Trainer and Speaker - Global Performance

"The information contained in this book has changed the way I set goals forever. Incredible!"

- Matt Adams
Sales Director, Niagara, Australia

"Scott has lifted the lid on what I see as possible."

- Johnny Glanville
Simcoe Tennis, Ontario, Canada

"Scott understands the way people think like no one I've ever met. He helped me create the change I needed that catapulted my income by 800%. I feel more successful than I ever have and I am burning with enthusiasm for life."

- Ian Bellion
National Sales Manager, Australia

"Scott has managed to combine years of relevant experience with years of specific research to reveal a natural and powerful method to achieve one's dreams."

- Stephen Whitehouse
Entrepreneur, Coach, Musician U.K.

My cousin highly recommended your book, which has had a MASSIVE impact on me! I've been reading self development books for 20 years and yours is a game changer! Much like Dale Carnegies "How to win friends.." was for me 20 years ago. Have just finished reading the book for the second time in 6 months. I've actually had a few close business colleagues read it on my recommendation too. I've been likening it to a modern day 'Think and Grow Rich', which I have read a few times. It is amazing but the language makes it harder to grasp the concepts. I also like that your book delves a bit deeper, I just can't speak more highly of it!

- Michelle Holt

Had to let you know, your book has changed my life! I'm setting goals I believe and truly moving forward for the first time. I used to set goals and freak out, not now. Thank you !!

- Hannah Stowe

The POWER *of* SUBCONSCIOUS GOAL SETTING

SCOTT GROVES

www.scottgroves.com

Published by:

Scott Groves International
ScottGroves.com

Burleigh Heads, Queensland
Australia 4220

All correspondence to the publisher
at the above address.

Revised Cover Design by Energize Design
energizedesign.com

All enquiries to the publisher.

ISBN 978-0-9751198-0-8

Category: Self Help: Personal Success: Business: Author

ScottGroves.com

To my beautiful children Annabel, Andre & Teddy…

Forever chase your dreams!

&

To those who seek the emotional, spiritual, physical and financial abundance that is your birthright.

Thank You

"If only my hand could express what's in my heart."

As this is the Second Edition, I will never forget the contribution, effort and time put into this book by so many key people. Because of this, much of the book itself, along with the "Thank you's" remain unchanged.

To Johnny Glanville, always my chief editor on this book, and the best friend anyone could ask for. Johnny toiled away with me on 36 re-writes and drafts of this before it became what you hold in your hands today. He is a champion human being and a lifelong friend. Johnny, your commitment to this book and the help you have given me leaves me speechless and will never be forgotten. You are one of a kind. The world is a better place for having you here.

To John Kanary, thank you for taking the time to contribute to this book. I learned from every conversation we shared. You are an amazing man that I am grateful to know.

To John Bannister and the Team at Joshua Books (1st Edition), thank you for all of your advice and work. Most of all, thanks for your belief in this book. Your desire to see humanity lifted with a message like this added to the drive in me to create something we could all be proud of.

To Ian Bellion, I have loved watching you live this message. Thank you for your belief in me and this book - I always feel it.

To Matt Adams, thank you for being there. Your pragmatism and focus has served as a great example for me. The best friend a mate could ask for.

Special thanks to John Kanary, Bob Proctor, Mark Victor Hansen, Jim Rohn, Les Brown, Anthony Robbins and Brian Tracy - you've inspired me for over 20 years. May your genius live on.

To You, the Readers
A cool, like-minded group of goal setters from over 30+ countries around the world who have taken the time to write and email me with such open and honest accounts of the insights, transformations and results you've experienced from this material truly leaves me humbled.

I always endeavour to personally respond as many of you know. I can honestly tell you that if it wasn't for you, I probably would not be updating this book and re-releasing it - a heartfelt thanks!

***

To Missy, you have given me a second life of meaning and inspiration. You are my breath of fresh air every day.

Finally, to my Mum and Dad - thank you for giving me the freedom to explore this world.

I remember the day the first paperbacks landed and I signed a copy and sent you both one. It feels strange now writing this to you since you have both passed away. But I sit here now with your copy on my desk Mum, and as I go about the re-writes and I am reminded by your void - just how precious life is.

I miss you both xo

"It's not how long you live, it's HOW you live."

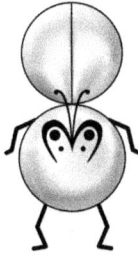

Contents

Special Introduction by John Kanary
International Best Selling Author
of
"Breaking Through Limitations"

What if one idea in this book could move your life to a new level of living?

What if all you had to do was read and apply one chapter a week to achieve a better quality of life?

One evening while relaxing in my study, I received a phone call from Scott Groves and he said he was referred to me by Mark Neil, a name that will always get my attention and blessing for anyone using it as a reference.

Scott asked me to write the introduction to this book. I thanked him for such an honour however, I would prefer if we met first. Scott lives in Australia and I live in Canada but I would be in Australia within the next two weeks so we decided we would meet and I would get his book then.

Scott and I did meet; in fact, I spent (invested) two days with this young man and came away with a real feeling that I had just met a person who will have a profound impact on the world. I felt tremendous power from this young man's innocence and sincerity.

I left Australia with Scott's book to read on my flight to British Columbia, Canada and what I found in the book is very consistent with what I found in Scott. I also found an absolutely perfect formula to connect your goals with the subconscious mind and most importantly, a very clear understanding of what people want to achieve and the beliefs opposing them in the subconscious mind - those hidden programs and scripts that we must become aware of whether we are going to move ahead in our lives.

I usually don't give people advice - I will either suggest or guide people to certain tools so, if you find yourself stuck in life's gap, "The Power of Subconscious Goal Setting" is the bridge between where you are to where you want to be.

Create some fire and pass the torch.

John Kanary
President, Life Success Coach Inc.

Where It All Began

The "16 Year Old" Letter

I still remember the day I received the letter in the mail that made me realise that this book just had to be written. I had been working hard on myself for many years, reading books, listening to tapes and going to seminars when I opened the letter that gave me the clarity I needed.

The letter was from a thirteen year old boy who had a high school teacher that made the class write down some of the things they wanted to do when they left school. The young boy probably wouldn't have written such a letter if it wasn't for the teachers prompting. It was an A4 sheet of paper that was filled with dreams that would seem well beyond what most people ever achieve in a lifetime. To a thirteen year old boy though, there is no such thing as impossible, so he just wrote.

"A job I would be keen to do when I leave school. I think I would have to turn pro (tennis) and travel the circuits if I'm good enough."

As I read through the letter I stopped for a moment to refer to the note which was attached from the boy's mother. She wrote on it, *"I don't think my son would realise it but 90% of these things have been accomplished"*.

She was right. How do I know she was right? That thirteen year old boy was me.

That letter took sixteen years to arrive at my door. You can imagine the nostalgic feelings that I experienced as I began to reflect on my achievements. I am grateful that my mother had an incredible knack for accumulating family history. All but two goals on this piece of paper have been achieved and in case you were wondering, the other two are happening right now because you are reading this book. My heartfelt thanks go to you.

The strong message that this letter drove home for me was that the power of the subconscious mind will never quit until it manifests its goal, no matter how long it takes. The lesson which I now really understood was that the subconscious will accept the written word as a command and go about creating the actual fact with or without our conscious awareness.

The Power of Subconscious Goal Setting had never been clearer to me. As a boy without any apparent limitations, I was amazed at how accurate this letter reflected my life up until now. I don't remember ever writing it, but reading through it brought a flood of memories back to me. The most important things in this letter are the things I am most proud of today.

From the age of seventeen I had worked as a tennis coach whilst pursuing my own dreams of playing professional tennis. My job as a coach was to bring the best out of my students. To find ways to develop them as quickly as I could into the type of player or person that they wanted to become. It was the beginning of the most rewarding times of my life. I had a responsibility to the people I coached that caused me to ask questions like-

- "What makes people successful?"
- "Why do some people seem to do so much better than others, no matter how hard they seem to try?"
- "What is the common denominator of success and how can others apply this knowledge?"

Questions you may have even asked yourself from time to time.

These questions have resulted in a fourteen year search which has brought us together today. It has been a journey of joy and anguish, excitement and pain, victory and disappointments. However life experience can be learned in no other school than the school of life.

Life's Questions

Throughout life we all take stock at times to sit back and ponder why we are here. Sometimes it is out of necessity when our backs are to the wall. Other times it is through our personal reflection as we take in the lives of those around us and look back and forward to some of our own dreams.

The purpose of writing this book is to share my ideas and what I have learned about the power of the subconscious and how that relates to the achievement of one's goals. I will also share the way goals affect us and how we subconsciously influence the outcomes we so often seek. There is often conflict between what goals we would really like to accomplish and the subconscious programming that directs our lives and every behaviour and decision we engage in.

Through developing a greater understanding of the mind over the years I have come to learn some things about goal setting and how the subconscious plays its vital part. Things like dealing with our own limiting thoughts and how to overcome our own doubts and fears. How to handle rejection and maintain our self-esteem when the world is telling us to *"be realistic"*.

Regardless of what it is you want in life, *The Power of Subconscious Goal Setting* is a comprehensive success strategy that you can apply to any area of your life. It will help you to see fears and doubts for what they really are. It will allow you to search deep inside yourself for what it is you really want and lay out a *'Murphy Proof Plan'* so that you can achieve it.

In the back of most people's minds is that special 'something' which they secretly or not so secretly harbour that they would really like to experience.

Have you have ever had the experience of starting out towards a goal and three months later found that you no longer really desired it? In this book you will find the underlying reasons for this and a method for overcoming it. It is a lesson of such significance that it could literally save you years of your life.

If you have ever talked yourself out of doing something great or allowed other people to convince you to not try then you are not alone. I have personally been there and I will share what I have learned about how to deal with this with the *'Rejection See Saw'*.

Throughout the countless conversations I have had with people regarding goals I have noticed that goals have somehow attracted a kind of stigma. I have seen people cringe when asked, *"what are your goals?"* I have seen salespeople turn up to the Monday morning meetings only to find the subject is goal setting and they automatically feel like they have wasted their time. It made me begin to wonder what causes this stigma with goals.

Is it possible that some people have proved to themselves that goals don't work? Is it the constant failure in pursuit of their dreams that has caused them to give up on the goal and themselves? *The Power of Subconscious Goal Setting* will help you build a foundation that will cause your goal setting ability to go to heights you may never have experienced.

Decide In Advance

It will be the serious students of their own personal lives who will reap the greatest rewards when reading this book. I want you to decide in advance, right now the approach you are going to take with this book.

What you decide will determine how you approach this book. My obligation to you is to *'Walk the talk'* when it comes to goal setting. In order for me to be thorough in my approach I want you to ask yourself three questions. I would recommend answering these in writing for yourself. Doing so will give you tremendous clarity. Goal setting itself is about clarity. The greater the clarity you have the more you will get out of this book and the natural consequence of this will mean you get more out of life.

Here are your questions -

1. What is the purpose of reading this book?
2. What do you want to experience whilst reading this?
3. What do you want to learn?

Whether you are already a high achiever or struggling to make ends meet in a job you don't like makes no difference. *The Law of Futurity* states that, *"It doesn't matter where you're coming from; it only matters where you're going"*. Goal setting has nothing to do with where you are coming from or what may have happened to you in the past. What really matters is the direction you are going from this day on. There is absolutely no question that goals are the life-changing tool that is required to take you from where you are, to where it is you want to go.

"If you don't know where you're going then any road will get you nowhere." - *Henry Kissinger*

People who are succeeding will tell you that it is goals that have had the single biggest impact on their lives. It is one of the least understood skills on this planet. It is rarely taught in schools or discussed at the dinner tables of this world. Even the majority of workplaces fail to teach their employees how to set and achieve goals.

Goal setting, like any other program or technique has continued to develop over the years. The days of writing a goal down, putting a date on it and going for it are gone. In the society we live in today we are faced with an enormous amount of input unlike what our ancestors used to experience. This input is mainly from the internet and television. The violence, drugs and world events of today are shaping our minds in such different ways. We can sit and watch terrorist acts as it is actually happening. These sorts of things were never witnessed first hand years ago. Technology has changed many things. The affects on us subconsciously is the most powerful of all. People are developing more fears than ever and subconsciously, even as infants we are taking in information, for better or for worse that we have never previously faced.

The Power of Subconscious Goal Setting involves a process of overcoming fears, limiting beliefs and subconscious images that we may have inadvertently picked up from our external environment.

It will show you unique ways to free your mind and move forward along a path of truth. As you journey along this path you may be tricked into believing in the circumstances which overshadow this truth. Remember that things are not as they appear to be. Discovering this truth means that we can begin to look deep into what we really want without experiencing fears and doubts. These are normally conjured up when one begins to consider the seriousness of following through on their dreams.

> *"Understanding casts the shadow of our circumstances behind us." - Scott Groves*

If you are willing and are looking for a way to go to another level then I welcome you to the next evolution of goal achievement. I am sure it won't be the last. The human race is yet to tap the potential that is housed within our wonderful minds. With patience, application and time you will see what I mean. I don't expect anyone who has never set and pursued goals before to believe in the power of them in the beginning. It takes time to develop the faith and understanding. Each step in this book is a self mastery course in itself.

Keeping your mind open to what's possible is where you'll discover your deep reservoir. If you must doubt anything then I ask you to *doubt what you doubt*.

I remember sharing these principles with someone who was over sixty years of age who was working in the direct sales industry on commission only. She had extreme difficulty in putting pen to paper because she didn't believe she could achieve what she wanted to write down. Once she began to *doubt her doubts* she went on to make close to $30,000 in six weeks when in the three months previous had failed to make $6000. Anyone can do this and you are never too old or too young to start. The fact is that we are setting images in our minds of the outcomes we expect all the time. We are born goal seeking organisms. We are unlike any other part of creation and our minds have the unique ability to bring into reality that which is consistent with our subconscious conditioning. *The Power of Subconscious Goal Setting* is so powerful that it prevents the conscious rejection of an idea by retarding doubt. Doubt that many people begin to experience before they have even finished writing down what it is they want.

This book is structured in a way that will walk you through a series of questions. A systematic way to build a foundation that starts from the deepest levels of the subconscious and works steadily back to a level of conscious awareness. This will allow you to discover what it is you truly want and what you are truly capable of achieving.

Each step of this book is built around the successful layering of exercises and thought patterns so the subconscious patterns you may have played out in the past don't interfere with your success in the future.

Stay open minded to some of the things that may have caused you some anguish and frustrations with pursuing your goals in the past and you will recognise how to overcome these without torment. The more positive and successful you are already, the faster you will take action on the ideas presented in this book. This book has been written with the purpose of changing lives. To do this, it is best that you see it as a 100% ACTION book. This book is not to be read from front to back and put down on a shelf with a reflective, "Oh that had some good ideas in it". This book is to be ACTIVELY EXPERIENCED. A wise philosopher once said,

"To know, and not to do, is not to know."

If you are serious about setting goals and truly want to change your life then you will complete each task ahead to the best of your ability. As you grow, your best today will be the benchmark for tomorrow. What you achieved in the past is only a reflection of your potential. I have met many people who believe that what they have achieved in the past is the ceiling on their ability. The truth is that it is only a glimpse. It is the first step to something greater. Give yourself the necessary time to develop these abilities and you will see what I mean.

You and no one else will know what you are really capable of until you take the time to set some really important goals.

"We can fool everyone but ourselves."

I have written this book in a way so that some ideas will leap out at you while others will lay sleeping waiting for your growth to recognise them. The mother of learning is the repetition of a good idea. Many of you will need to take the time to internalise the information presented in this book and the only way to really internalise is by doing. All truly successful people take action on a good idea.

The joy I have in writing a book like this is that it gets another opportunity to prove itself in the toughest testing ground of all. Information like this belongs amongst the high achievers of this world. Because you have such a book in your hands just proves that you have what it takes. You already are amongst the top 10% of people in society who take the necessary time and make the necessary effort to grow. I estimate that 90% of people will walk straight by the bookshelf that you found this on and pick up the latest TV magazine so they can plan their week of TV watching. For as long as I am on this planet, this is a percentage that I am determined to change. Congratulate yourself on taking the time to place something in your hands that designs lives and can bring you all you dream of. Give yourself time to grow and with the repetition of each idea your understanding of these principles will grow with you.

You have probably had the experience of reading a book or watching a movie and seeing something in it that you didn't notice the first time around. This isn't to say that it wasn't there before. What you have now found is something within yourself that wasn't there before. It is an indicator of how much you have grown as a person. Each and every time you go over ideas such as the ones presented in this book you begin from a new level of awareness.

Studies show that when you set goals you will increase your income; in fact you can retire financially free instead of being dependant on government pensions and handouts like millions of people worldwide. You will have more satisfying relationships. You will experience greater health and perhaps even extend your life. Focus your attention on enjoying the journey. The excitement of anticipation is gone once you've arrived at your destination.

The Concept

The Power of Subconscious Goal Setting is about setting an image of potential in the subconscious and allowing the subconscious to go about the achievement of your goal. We do this by looking at three levels of the subconscious and we start with the deepest subconscious level that is the furthest from our conscious awareness. The reason we do this is because most people set goals consciously and they never consider the subconscious conditioning of the past that may be holding them back. This gap between what people want to achieve and what they subconsciously believe themselves capable of causes doubt, fear, anxiety and a whole heap of other negative emotions. Achieving goals is supposed to be fun and exciting. So instead of spending years trying to bridge the gap between where you are and where you want to be, let's start by setting an image that the subconscious acts on and doesn't consciously reject with a thought like, *"I could never do that"*.

The first subconscious level we are going to explore is that of the identity. We will do this by using the gift of responsibility that we each develop as we enter the ages of eight, nine, ten and above.

The next level has to do with values. In *The Power of Subconscious Goal Setting* your values will be used to bridge the gap on your goals. This makes certain that years aren't wasted on goals that aren't important.

The third level, which is the closest to conscious awareness of the three, is the area of beliefs. With each of the above we will go into details in their specific chapters.

As you journey through this book, each chapter will bring your goals and what you are really put on this earth for, what would really give you the most fulfilment in life, and what you are really capable of achieving, closer to your level of conscious awareness. And I will help you to achieve them by getting absolute congruency *between* your values and beliefs.

Tips for Getting the Most Out of this Book

If you wish to get the most out of this book there are a couple of suggestions I have for you that you may want to take on board. Throughout the book you will hear me repeat myself, particularly when it comes to completing the exercises. Since you cannot hear my voice I want you to know that I am speaking to you with an encouraging voice, urging you to go for it and take action. We all have an inner voice of the writer that plays in our heads when we read. I am strong in my desire to see you get the most out of this book. I want you to picture me with you as we take each step together.

Here are seven tips you can apply to really get the most out of this book.

Note: You would have probably noticed already that the pages are left aligned rather than justified like most other books. This is done intentionally as the jagged right edge causes less strain on your eyes and allows you take in the information with greater ease. Your eyes will find it easier to track the page and flow from line to line. Enjoy!

1. Keep an open mind. I will be presenting you some concepts that you may or may not be familiar with. Some of them may be very challenging or confronting as you look deep into yourself. As your mind expands and stretches, it naturally becomes easier. Keep an open mind and be patient.

2. Highlight key points (use different colors each time you re-read a section). I highlight in every book I read. It is the fastest way to go back over the things that had the most impact on me. When it comes to re-reading the book or certain sections I can see how I've grown because I begin to notice different key points. The old highlights appear to become a part of me. As you review the ideas that mean the most to you, you will begin to notice over time how comfortably they begin to sit with you. Becoming comfortable with a higher idea is a critical factor when it comes to achieving your goals.

3. Do the obvious. Complete the exercises.

4. Take your time. There is no rush to complete this book. It is not a race. Do it excellent and right. The disciplines you begin to take as you read this book will lay the foundation of your future. If you are not consciously creating new empowering habits then you are reinforcing old unproductive ones.

5. Explain the key principles to someone else. An old teaching philosophy says that you don't really understand something until you can explain it to someone else so that they understand it. This is a great way to see how you've grown.

6. Translate ideas that pop into your mind into your own words. This is kind of the written version of Tip no.5. It works well because when you don't have the opportunity to dialogue with someone else; it is like discussing it on your own.

7. As you read ask yourself, "*How does this apply to me?*" The more you apply these principles to your own life the more you will get out of this book.

Let's GO !

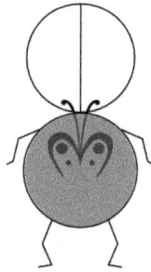

CHAPTER 1

The Mind

"It all begins in the mind."

The Power of Subconscious Goal Setting is about setting goals in a way that they burn themselves into the subconscious so that every action and decision is made in harmony with our inner core. The greater your understanding of the mind as it relates to the achievement of your goals the greater your possibilities.

The most powerful computer in the world is contained between your two ears. Experts claim that to build a computer that has the same capacity as the human mind would be as big as three Empire State buildings. Think about that for a moment. We are creatures of limitless natures. The challenge with being born into a world that is abundant with potential and opportunity is that we are given a mind without an instruction manual.

Over time society has learned to believe in a scarcity mentality. One where opportunities are limited and abundance is reserved for the minority. Studies have indicated that we fail to use even one tenth of the potential that is housed within our brains. I once read the post mortem excerpts of Einstein which showed neural pathway connections did not quite reach 10% of his brain area. The potential is limitless. As you begin to see the abundance that exists and the truth that is disguised by circumstance, you will be using the

Universal Mind as it was intended. You will have at your disposal a potent force that creates realities of choice.

Universal Mind

The Universal Mind is what makes humans the same. We are an energy that transcends every part of this universe. There is a Universal Law that says, "Everything is energy". Every single molecule on this earth is energy. This energy vibrates at different rates in harmony with the form it is taking on. H_2O for example will form the matter of water at a certain rate of vibration. The speed of this vibration is known as frequency. If we slow down the frequency of H_2O it will take on the form of ice. If we increase the frequency, the H_2O will move through the formation of water and eventually become steam. This change of form will cause the H_2O to evaporate into the universe. And even though we may not always visibly see steam, on some level we know that it exists.

Thought is one of the highest forms of vibration in this universe. As the rate of vibration increases with your thoughts, so does the potency of its force.

It is this function of the *Universal Mind* that makes us the same. How we use these functions is what makes us different. As humans we each differ in our lives based on how we use these Universal Laws. Many of them will be discussed throughout this book. As you increase your understanding with each of these laws you will naturally begin to see ways in which you can create the life of your choice.

At the beginning of each chapter you will see the model that I use to visually describe how the Universal Mind works. Much of what we will be discussing in this book is based around tapping the storehouse of potential contained within your subconscious mind. The subconscious is the doorway to your potential. Unlock it, and you unlock a force from within you that allows you to live your life on any level you choose.

The Universal Mind basically has two parts. The upper circle (head) I refer to as the Conscious Mind. The lower circle (body) I refer to as the Subconscious Mind. I do this purposefully to prevent us from thinking of the subconscious as something that is just contained within the head. Its energy is universal.

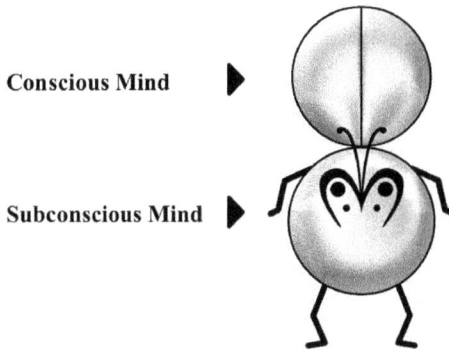

The Subconscious Model uses the shape of the butterfly to symbolize the heart so that we are reminded of the powerful effect emotions have on our subconscious. It is the emotional involvement in an idea that is held in the conscious mind that allows the manifestation of that idea to begin its creation. The antennae of the butterfly are receptive to what comes from the conscious mind through to the subconscious. Emotion is the conductive force.

The conscious mind itself has two parts. The two parts represented in the head of our model are the Inductive Conscious Mind (left) and the Deductive Conscious Mind (right).

The subconscious *is* universal. It penetrates every cell in your body giving you muscle memory, causing your heart to beat, lungs to breathe and a whole host of other things without any conscious thought. It even goes beyond the body to the point where we begin to attract people through this potency of emotional thought.

You may have had the experience of thinking about a friend who you haven't seen or heard from in a while. The thoughts about your friend are intense and frequent. And surprise, surprise, within the next 24 hours they have phoned you. People who don't yet fully understand some of the most basic *Universal Laws* would call that a 'coincidence'. I have come to believe that there is no such thing as coincidence. Everything happens for a reason. Everything has an underlying cause. We call this law, the *Law of Cause and Effect*.

Just like the physical laws that exist in this world that govern things such as gravity, electricity, water and all physical matter, so too are there scientific laws that govern thought.

Coincidence?

Some years ago I was working in sales when I had a unique opportunity to give these laws the acid test. I left one of our regular sales meetings and headed off to my first appointment for the day when I realised that I had forgotten to charge my mobile phone. Our sales system worked in a way that when we made a sale we needed to phone our order in immediately for installation purposes or we greatly risked losing the deal. This could mean jeopardising anywhere from $500 to over $1000 in commission in one day.

Driving towards my first appointment I received a call and my phone went dead immediately and I didn't have my car charger. I didn't panic or even allow my mind to begin to explore the negative consequences. I had a surreal peace and tranquillity that everything would turn out for the best and I truly expected it.

I was literally five minutes from my first appointment and I drove to a local pawn shop to see if they had a car charger but there wasn't any that fit my type of phone. I pulled up at a set of lights about 500 metres from this house still calm and expectant of a positive outcome when all of a sudden a friend of mine named Greg pulled up at the lights in the left turn lane exactly level with my car. Both of our windows were down which was strange for me since I normally travel with air conditioning running. We looked at each other and I said "*Hey, do you have a car charger for a Nokia?*" Without hesitating he threw it in through my window, the lights turned green and he drove off to the left and I went straight ahead to my first appointment. Coincidence... I think not.

I began laughing as I drove away but the story doesn't end there. The first house I went to I sold. What made this even more amazing was that in a country like Australia where virtually everyone has a phone, this first house I sold to ... did not.

Looking back I truly believe that had I allowed myself to get upset and frustrated then none of this would have worked out the way it did. The chances of meeting Greg, with the right charger in that sliver of time before going to a house that didn't have a phone where I would have definitely needed one is too great.

The Law of Expectations says that
"We get in life, what we expect to get".

Everything Begins With Thought

You cannot look at a single man made object on this entire planet and not find something that didn't begin as a thought. Everywhere you look you will see objects that have manifested from thought into what we experience everyday.

Any thought accepted by the subconscious mind will manifest into its physical form. Every single result you have experienced up until now is the result of the thinking that has gone on in your mind. Your body will consistently produce actions in harmony with the images that are held within your subconscious. If you wish to change some of the results you are getting in your life then you need to begin by changing your thoughts.

Circle of Comfort

When we attempt something beyond what we have previously experienced and begin to think in ways that stretch our normal thinking we take ourselves out of our *Circle of Comfort*. This is where we enter a world that is unfamiliar to us. Our previous conditioning has no recollection and has no experience to draw on. That is why people experience anxiety, excitement and many other emotions when on the verge of something new.

It is outside this *Circle of Comfort* that we experience feelings of discomfort as we stretch. Each time we persist through this discomfort we begin to expand our *Circle of Comfort*. We create within ourselves the ability to handle different situations and circumstances. We literally grow our capacity to be comfortable with a greater range of things. What we as adults must realise or re-learn is that this growth is a natural expansion of ourselves. It is inherently built into us so that we can go on to do whatever we want to.

As children I am sure many of us engaged in this natural expansion of our *Circle of Comfort* without even thinking. It is a lesson so simple that most people have unlearned it growing older. Somehow people have let their *Circle of Comfort* become resistant to the expansion. Imagine if we had taken this limiting approach to life when learning to walk, ride a bike or even drive a car. We would look funny as a bunch of adults crawling to work in our uniforms and suits wouldn't we?

The truth is that although pretty much everybody walks, many people are mentally crawling through life, afraid to stand tall and reach up for the metaphorical cookie jar which is full of the sweet things in life. The paradox is that in order to be successful we must learn to become childlike again. We must continue to grow and try new things without fear. All good parents encourage their children to "*get back on the bike*", yet with age we talk ourselves out of the thrill of experiencing new things.

The great challenge with this discomfort is the labels which we give it. What would normally be a natural state of growth can be mentally twisted into feelings of fear, doubt and worry.

Here's how it can happen...

You get offered a career move that has huge potential pay-off and simultaneously carries some risk. You experience a frequency (a physical vibration - discomfort) that you are not accustomed to because you have worked in a steady job for the past five years and your security appears solid. You feel this frequency in your body and in an effort to understand it, you attempt to label it. Let's say you have called the discomfort "*fear*". If you accept the risk of this new opportunity your security could be under threat and you may feel like your survival is at stake. Your label is subconsciously interpreted as a fear for your survival and your primitive brain takes over with its fight or flight mechanism and you back away from the opportunity.

Our Circle of Comfort must be recognised for what it is. This is an important point so grab a highlighter.

> **"Our Circle of Comfort is what we have allowed ourselves to get used to."**

How different would your behaviour have been had you labelled this frequency as arousal or excitement? Does the label we give our emotions determine the actual emotion we feel? Does this explain why some people move forward in the face of uncertainty whilst others scurry for the safety of comfort? I will answer the question on labelling our emotions in the chapter on self-talk.

> **Psychologists worldwide often talk about how we are born with only two fears. Fear of falling and fear of loud sounds while all other fears are learned. I challenge this. I have raised 3 children of my own and believe that falling is a learned fear also. We are only born with the fear of loud sounds.**

Emotions

"What you have in your heart, you can hold in your hand."
- Scott Groves

The Ancient Greeks used to refer to the subconscious as *"The Heart"*. They knew the powerful effect emotions had on the subconscious. Even Ancient Egyptians when mummifying a body would remove all of the internal organs except the heart. They believed that the heart held the secret to the soul and it would be needed in the next life.

As human beings we are naturally goal seeking organisms that have the ability to create the reality which *we feel* most intensely about.

The heart is where we commonly refer to feeling emotions. It is these emotions that have a powerful influence on the subconscious. If you give your mind highly charged emotional input it can be accepted very quickly. This is why traumatic events can have such an enormous impact on people. The term *"Take it to Heart"* begins to make more sense.

I vividly recall an experience as a 12 year old boy when I visiting my father in hospital. For the past six years Dad had been in and out of hospitals with what was yet to be identified as Chronic Pancreatitis. The conversations on our visits varied depending on the

state of Dad's health. Sometimes there was little said. Just the
attendance of my Mum, my sister Jodie and I seemed to be comfort
enough when he wasn't well. This one occasion occurred when Dad
and I were alone together. Mum and Jodie had gone for a walk to the
hospital kiosk for some lollies that Dad could eat between the bland
hospital meals he'd grown tired of. Dad and I began talking about the
cross country race I was to run the following day. It was an Inter
School race that combined a dozen schools in the region. I was
always competitive in most sports but I only really ever shined at
soccer and tennis. I guess Dad sensed that Mum and Jodie were just
minutes from returning. He leaned over to me with a look of deep
conviction and said, "*Son, bring me up a trophy and go and win it for
me tomorrow*". I could feel his eye contact penetrate to the depths of
my soul.

I can admit to having mixed feelings as I looked my father in
the eyes as he lay there in his cold, sterile hospital bed. What was I
supposed to say to him? There were so many runners better than I
was. I wanted to win that trophy for him more than anything in the
world.

I didn't make any promises as I left the hospital that evening
but in my mind the seed had been planted. I felt a burning desire to
win. An intensity like nothing I had felt up to this point in my life. I
was going to go out there and give this cross country race everything
I had. I couldn't bare to give Dad news of anything other than
winning. I could see his face non-stop from the moment I left the
hospital until the finish line the next day. For 10 minutes and 23
seconds I ran like my life depended on it. I ran like my fathers life
depended on it. There wasn't a 12 year old running that day who
wanted to win as much as I did. That night at the hospital I handed
my father a trophy with a shiny engraved gold plate that read... 1st
place. For as long as I live I will always remember the feelings
associated with this experience. I remember it like it was yesterday.
How an intense burning desire can be created with one request from
someone who means so much to you. It is a lesson that I carry with
me to this day.

"Nothing is small if it's significant."

Some people's lives have been dramatically changed by as little as one highly emotional event. This can be both positive and negative. The negative emotional experiences are many and varied. They can be either physical or emotional traumas.

Positive emotional input can leave an imprint on the subconscious just as powerful. This is why achieving success in one important area of your life can give you the feeling of being programmed with success forever. When you feel something with all of your heart it becomes difficult to persuade you to feel differently. Success and what you feel you are capable of is no different.

If you know someone who has always wanted an abundance of wealth but when they talk about it, all you hear is defeat. It's like listening to a monotone old record playing with a singer who's been totally sapped of all zest for life. There's no emotional involvement in the idea of becoming wealthy and ultimately, their results and bank account will reflect this.

Your body will only ever produce results consistent with what is emotionally passed over to the subconscious.

The more intense the emotional involvement then the stronger the influence on the subconscious mind will be. Take a sportsperson who harbours two very powerful emotions. If they love winning more than they hate losing then the dominant emotion is love. A very positive emotion such as love is a powerful influence. Imagine the difference if an athlete hated losing more than they loved winning. Do you think the dominant emotion of hate would have a bearing on their results and the way they feel when they are involved in competition? You bet it would.

The use of emotional involvement is also evident in people who talk about their fears. They do so in such a way that the fear becomes reinforced rather than resolved. Fears can be highly emotional and just talking about them can raise one's blood pressure. This once again is the body's response to what is held in the subconscious. You would already be aware of the now common knowledge that stress is directly attributed to heart attacks. We must never underestimate the power of the subconscious and the effect that emotions have on it.

CONSCIOUS MIND

There are two primary workings in the conscious mind. The first is the ability to accept or reject an idea. The second is that the conscious mind can only hold one thought at a time. Let's explore these now.

How to Use the Rebel in Us All

When we were growing up; other people had the ability to put things into our subconscious minds. As youngsters, our brains hadn't developed to the point where we could distinguish what was best for us or to understand certain concepts or events. Under the age of ten, it is very rare to see a child grasp the concepts that we are discussing here regarding the conscious and subconscious.

What that means is that as we were growing up we believed what we were told and acted on what we believed. Many people can share stories with you about their third generation of doctors, lawyers or carpenters. The people we associated with the most are the ones who influenced our Thinking and beliefs the most. We unconsciously inherited the attitudes and beliefs about life from people close to us like parents, school teachers and guardians.

Eventually we all reach an age where we can begin making our own decisions. It is around about the age of eight or nine that we began to get a sense of who we are. Our own identity if you will.

Generally it's not until we begin getting embarrassed by our parents at around eleven to thirteen years of age that we have sufficiently developed the ability to grasp the concept of the conscious and subconscious. It is in this stage of growth that we begin to reject the advice of our parents and rebel against our school teachers. This rebellion is a sign that someone is developing the ability to reason. They begin to question what they hear and see rather than accepting everything as *"This is the way it is"*. It is a very healthy time in someone's life if they are taught how to apply it effectively. Instead of looking upon what I jokingly call the 'teenage rebellion movement' as a negative, as a society we should be educating teenagers on the new power they now have at their disposal.

Each of us should continue to develop the rebel within us all. Reject thoughts that drag us away from the life we desire. Use our power of conscious choice to make decisions that empower the lives of us and others.

One at a Time

Let's discuss the application of the second principle where the conscious mind can only hold one thought at a time. This means it is impossible to harbour negative thoughts whilst thinking of something positive. We cannot simultaneously worry and feel confident at the same time. We cannot feel courageous and scared at the same time. We also cannot believe and have doubt at the same time. You cannot concentrate whilst you are pre-occupied. Conscious input is what programs our subconscious minds.

"Everything starts on a conscious level. Everything happens on a
subconscious level." - *John Kanary*

If you are the type of person who is still worrying about how you're going to pay the monthly bills then your dominant thoughts will create feelings of insecurity, anxiety and fear. The ultimate result will be leaving you short of money at the end of the month.

Knowing that you can only hold one thought at a time you could probably begin to see what would happen if you were to substitute one thought for another. Goal setting has the effect of replacing negative thoughts with very positive ones.

In other words, replace the feelings of insecurity with positive expectation. Keep your mind focused *ON* what you want to achieve rather than the obstacles that *appear* to stand in your way. All of us need to overcome the challenges that life throws us in order to toughen us up for the big win. I remember attending a convention where Stef du Plessis was speaking and he said something that burned itself into my memory. It was,

"Lessons unlearned get repeated."

Ignoring worry, doubt and fear does not mean they will go away. You must substitute these for the emotions and thoughts that you would consistently like to experience. Consciously think about the positive outcome and your subconscious will go about its natural duty and find a way to create the actual fact.

Conscious Awareness

There are two parts to your conscious mind. Understanding these two parts will help you to understand why some people seem to *"go with the flow"* and do what everyone else is doing. Others go *"against the grain"* to set themselves apart in terms of what they achieve in life.

Deductive

In a deductive conscious state we automatically take on the energy that is in that environment. You would be familiar with this experience if you have ever walked into a room with a group of people who had been arguing, but hadn't personally witnessed it. Without becoming consciously aware of it you automatically become tense and uptight like those in the room. Through the *Law of Vibration* you begin to feel tension in your physical body. You feel it but you are not in a state of awareness that would describe what is happening. You literally become a product of the environment and begin to feel like everyone else in the room does. This is your deductive reasoning at work.

The opposite is also true. If you have ever been to a concert and as you walked in you felt the electricity. Everyone was having a great time. Even if you arrived in a very relaxed state, before long you would be feeling *'pumped'* like everyone else.

When you are presented with information in a deductive state it is automatically accepted by the subconscious as a command. It goes about shaping you without you even knowing it.

As children we are totally deductive. We accept virtually everything. If we grow up around people with limiting beliefs about wealth, who constantly discuss lack, then we tend to develop a similar picture of the world.

On the other hand, if we were to grow up around someone who believed anything was possible and abundance was all they spoke, you could imagine the difference.

In a deductive conscious state we will invariably become like those that we associate with. At one time or another we have probably all had the lecture about the type of friends we were hanging out with. People close to us would begin to see behavioural changes that even we were not aware of. We make the claim that we are still the same person but we are changing as a result of what we deductively are picking up.

Not only do we develop the same attitudes, beliefs, morals and values about things - we can even begin to talk like them. It's like surfers have a language of their own. If you study skateboarders, musicians, business people, sports people or oil riggers you will begin to notice the same.

Because each of us live with varied amounts of time in a deductive conscious state, who you associate with can play a big part in who you become.

Inductive

The inductive conscious state is where you have the ability to consciously accept or reject an idea. This is where you make choices. If we were to use the examples from above where the situations were the same you would instantly recognise them for what they were. You would recognise the tension or the amazing concert atmosphere. This inductive conscious state plays a crucial role in *The Power of Subconscious Goal Setting*.

This inductive conscious state has a higher awareness than your deductive state. This means that only what you consciously accept will be transferred to the subconscious. Any rejected thoughts will go into the trash heap.

This is a tremendous gift that once mastered will set you free. You may have had the experience where someone said something that you didn't agree with and you rejected it from your mind. A specific example would be, someone says something upsetting to you and you say to yourself, "I'm not going to let that upset me" as you turn and walk away.

An ingredient of success is developing the awareness of when you need to be in your inductive state or when you can allow yourself to *'switch off'*; thus becoming totally deductive to the world around you.

For example, when I am around some family members and even some friends, I make an effort to increase my inductive conscious awareness so that I can reject some of their attitudes about life. It's not to say that I don't love them because I do. The reason for this is because we have very different goals in life. For me to adopt some of their beliefs and attitudes about life would hinder what it is I'm achieving. This awareness also helps me to avoid stepping on their toes and pushing my values and beliefs down their throats.

A good time for me to go into a deductive conscious state is when I am around highly motivated goal achievers with a similar mindset. I am happy to pick up the attitudes that successful, happy, healthy, wealthy people have. Another good time for this is when I am watching a movie or walking along the beach. In these moments I like to just soak in the surroundings. Who wants to be in this high state of awareness all the time? Our conscious mind needs to take time out at some stage.

Understanding how to apply the two parts of the conscious mind to your life can move you rapidly towards the goals you seek.

Consciously Reject or Subconsciously Accept

The key distinction between the conscious mind and the subconscious is that the inductive conscious mind has the ability to accept and reject thoughts whilst the subconscious does not possess this ability. From this point on I will refer to this ability to accept or reject as the 'conscious mind' rather than writing 'inductive conscious mind'.

Whatever is accepted or not rejected by the conscious mind becomes planted in the subconscious like a seed in the garden. Many don't realise the importance of rejecting ideas that don't fit the reality of what they are trying to create. The seed deposited will produce its equivalent. In other words, good seeds produce good fruit, bad seeds produce bad fruit.

Slow down and take this in because there is a critical difference here that I want you to understand. Reject thoughts that aren't consistent with the reality you would like to create. Ignoring things does not normally mean they go away. Over time you will develop the ability to control your thoughts and consciously accept ideas and thoughts that support your desires and reject those which do not fit. In the beginning you must guard your mind carefully.

No Negative Trespassers Allowed

Only the healthy, wealthy, positive and wise are allowed in your garden. Consciously make the decision to accept the attitudes and beliefs of those around you or reject them from the game of life you're playing. Ignoring them means they will only sit on the sidelines sniggering at you waiting for something to go wrong. You must rise above this by getting them out of the stadium so you can assert yourself uninhibited.

SUBCONSCIOUS MIND

How to Program Your Automatic Goal Achiever

We have already discussed the enormous power that emotion has on the subconscious. The second way in which our thoughts pass through the door to the subconscious is through repetition. Any input repeated or focused upon over and over again will also be accepted by the subconscious and processed through its mental factory. This explains why people who constantly talk about what they *want* or *don't want* keep getting more of the same. When someone says, *"I don't want to think about the consequences of missing this car payment"* their mind will naturally become absorbed on the possible consequences.

We've all heard the one about the pink elephant. Don't think about a pink elephant. No matter what you are reading and whatever you do, keep your mind off a pink elephant. Don't see it or picture it in your mind whatever you do. Pardon the pun but do you get the picture?

We must understand that what is held in the conscious mind will be transferred to the subconscious. For the purpose of repetition I will reiterate, keep your mind *ON* what you want and keep your mind *OFF* what you don't want.

"We eliminate the effect of a negative circumstance when we begin thinking about what we do want."

We know that to learn anything requires repetition. Even the accelerated learning programs that help you to store massive pieces of information in short periods of time use repetition.

To master your thoughts will also require practice. Like driving a car we may feel awkward in the beginning but with repetitive practice we find ourselves driving without any conscious thought.

And once programmed, your success you will be as simple as turning the key to your car. Ask yourself, "Am I willing to take the time to set the pictures, thoughts and feelings of success that will attract to me what I seek?"

What You Say Is What You Get

The subconscious does not have a sense of humour. All of your humour is a conscious activity. What I mean by this is that you cannot jokingly tell yourself how stupid you are. Consciously we know we are not stupid but subconsciously it is a seed that becomes planted. The repetition of the word *'stupid'* can begin to shape the subconscious image we have of ourselves and leave us with our own self made consequences. When faced with a similar set of circumstances in the future we are more likely to act in the same habitual way due to the previous reinforcement. The fact that the word *'stupid'* came out of your mouth in the first place means it has been processed by the subconscious.

Remember that every action is an effect of what is held in your subconscious. That's where the saying, "*What you say is what you get*" comes from. As does Earl Nightingales, "*You get what you think about, most of the time*".

You Can't Beat the System

One of the most powerful lessons to be extracted from this book lies in understanding that what you hold in the subconscious mind grows and becomes the reality you will experience. When we put this into perspective with regards to goal setting, we want to introduce concepts, thoughts and ideas to the mind that we want accepted. Simultaneously we want to consciously reject thoughts and ideas that are not in harmony with the reality we want to create. If you want to attract more financial abundance then stopping telling your subconscious that *"You can't afford it"*. Instead ask your subconscious, *"How can I afford it?"* Think about words like abundance, wealth and prosperity. Let your mind become absorbed with these thoughts.

The subconscious holds the answer to any question you can ask it. It is an abundant treasure chest of wisdom. However it can only give you answers based on the questions you ask. If you ask questions like, *"How can I become financially independent and have fun in the process?"* your subconscious mind will find the answer.

Can you see the lesson here? Our questions direct our subconscious thinking. The quality of your questions will determine the quality of your life. *The Power of Subconscious Goal Setting* is an orderly series of questions. The old school of goal setting asks the question *WHAT* do you want and *WHEN* by. This *WHAT, WHEN* questioning approach creates doubt. Here's how...

Let's say you set a goal to *"Increase your income by 20% (WHAT) by December 21st next year (WHEN)"*. When you first set upon a goal with a specific timeline, your conscious mind has already made a judgement as to whether it believes achieving that goal within that timeframe is possible. This is usually based on past experiences. The subconscious has no experience of such a success in its infinite memory so the body begins to feel an energy called "doubt".

If the conscious mind rejects the possibility of a goal being achieved from the beginning then your challenge becomes trying to convince yourself to take action in the face of doubt. This method requires willpower in order to achieve your goal. You will in essence be fighting your own image of what you believe yourself capable. This is the danger of WHAT, WHEN questioning.

There is an absolute necessity for involving the subconscious in the process of goals. The root meaning of educate means to *"lead, bring, or draw out of"*.

WHAT, WHEN questioning is like ramming an idea into your mind hoping it will take root as you fight the weeds of doubt. This is not true education. True education would be opening the door through which your subconscious can express its infinite potential. Desire is the expression of an idea surfacing from within you. It is an expression of your potential.

True education is helping yourself develop the abilities and potential you already contain. Knowledge is the preparation required to unleash your potential. Application of knowledge is power.

24/7

The subconscious is like a factory that requires no manpower and never stops working. It works while you are awake and continues to work while you sleep. The subconscious holds the answer to every question you can ask it. This is why we so often hear of the decision-making process *'Sleep On It'*. Whatever is put through this mental factory will be produced 24 hours a day until it materialises in the world that we see and call *'reality'*.

We talked before about the subconscious requiring either repetition (duration) or emotion in order for it to be really affected. The conscious mind has the ability to turn ON and OFF. This ability to switch off is why we lose concentration.

The subconscious doesn't have to concern itself with concentration. It is relentless in its production and ruthless in its execution. Any thought held in the subconscious mind will be produced. You will notice I said *"will"*, not *'should be'* or *'could be'*.

An incredible amount has been learned about the subconscious over thousands of years. Understanding the subconscious is somewhat of a self-discovery and there isn't a book on this planet that will ever fully explain its possibilities. But each time you develop the ability to explain a *Universal Law* to someone else you will find within yourself a deeper understanding and further application for its use. An understanding that can only conclude - there are no limits and no boundaries.

Once programmed your subconscious will work 24/7 to help you bring about the reality you can see in your minds eye.

Vividly Imagined or Real

I have saved the best for last. This is without doubt my favourite law of them all.

The subconscious cannot tell the difference between something that is vividly imagined or real.

Let me explain with an example. Have you ever had the experience of drifting off to sleep and in your dream state you were walking along and all of a sudden you felt yourself mentally trip? Your leg shoots out to brace itself for the fall. Your entire body feels the jerk of your leg and you come to the conscious awareness that you were dreaming.

Your subconscious mind didn't know that you were dreaming. It thought that you were actually falling and in a split second it caused your body to respond.

What does this have to do with goal setting? Answer: Everything.

You can create mental pictures that are so vivid your mind will believe that it has already achieved your goal. Do you think it's easier to achieve great success the first time out, with no prior experience of that success or do you think it would be easier after you have already done it once and you simply had to do it again? We all know that once we have the absolute certainty of achieving our goal it would be much easier to repeat the success. Is this why many millionaires say that the second million is easier than the first?

Marathon - a Metaphor for Life!

Two friends of mine, Johnny and Louise have both ran marathons. I know both of them experienced gut-wrenching times during their 42 kilometre, bone jarring journeys. What I love is listening to the way they speak about running another one. It is so different now they know they have already completed one. They can vividly see themselves crossing the line. They can mentally trigger the feelings associated with their success. Isn't it possible they could have done this before their first race?

The truth is, that they both would have imagined what it would be like to cross the finish line. The greater the clarity they each visualised their outcome the less of a mental challenge it would've been. The physical aspect needs to be conquered each time a marathon is run but the mental needs to be conquered just once to give the certainty that it is possible.

For as long as I can remember, even back in my days playing pro tennis, I thought about what it would be like to run a marathon. In my mind, if I was being honest - it was impossible. Not impossible for humanity. Impossible for me!

But in my mid 30's, after accumulating a story most people could relate to - married, kids, work more, exercise less, put on weight, begin self-loathing for letting yourself go, etc - I decided to give triathlons a go. I started with short course triathlons. But first, came some training. I began running a bit. Got into the pool and back on the bike. I didn't even have a road bike so I chugged away on my cheap ass mountain bike that would double as a boat anchor it was so freakin' heavy.

Anyway, I got my first triathlon out of the way. It was hot. Getting off the bike to run I discovered a whole new definition of "jelly-legs". And it was great! What I got back was a long lost memory and feeling of competing. A bunch of new goals swept in.

After suckering my best mate Brett into some triathlons with me, we both got fitter. We both challenged each other. Trained together. And entered longer events.

We progressed to Olympic distance triathlons, half Ironman and even had some fun with off-road triathlons which is basically a swim in a swamp, mountain bike on rocky fire trails and a run in the mud. I was in heaven!

But there was one goal that kept entering my mind... the Marathon.

Was I seriously about to take on my "impossible"?

Pen to Paper is Good... Enter is Better!

When you want to get serious about a goal, write it down. That's the advice you normally hear. It's the advice I normally give. Except with physical goals. If you really want to commit, pay the fee and enter. Whether it's a gym, a program, a race - just enter. You're stuck then. The date is fixed. You know what time the gun goes off. You have every right to be excited because s#!t just got real. That's what entering the event does.

So early 2009 that's exactly what I did. Entry fee paid. Now what?

Pen to paper is good, but it's the next step after that really counts. The action the follows the goal setting creates momentum. And with momentum, commitment grows. You can only think about a goal so much. Achieving your impossible doesn't get any closer by writing it down a bunch of times. You have got to move.

Now the goal was clear, time for a plan - even a basic one would do. I started out with no clue. I thought you just had to run long all the time. Turns out you don't. Easy runs through the week of 6-10kms. Longer run on Sunday. Monday off each week. Gradually add kilometres but no more than 10% total km's per week. That was the plan. Simple enough in theory. Now comes the physical part.

Make Yourself

My 6 day a week running plan meant changes. Get out of bed earlier. Eat better. Learn about recovery and actually do it. 5am never sounds sexy but damn you can achieve a lot in life by making yourself get up at 5. You get hours to knock things over that lead you closer to your goals before most people are even out of bed. And when you do it consistently, there's a part of you that knows that. You are doing more than what most people are prepared to do. Every successful person understands this concept.

18 weeks of discipline is all it took for me to get ready. Some days were easy. Some hard. Really hard. Nutrition mistakes in long runs make you feel like you're either going to die, pass out or vomit. Running on legs so tired that you just want to go back to bed is part of it. But none of this lasts. You learn. You get stronger. And like me, you suddenly begin to believe in "impossible".

If you can accumulate enough wins - get up early, complete the weeks training, eat your broccoli - then impossible begins to look like "maybe I can do this".

July 2009 came quickly. I was nervous but felt ready. Gold Coast Marathon is my home event and it's one of the most competitive in the world with a mecca of Kenyans, Ethiopians and world class Japanese runners that I won't see until they come back past on their way home.

Australian legend Robert DeCastella is the race announcer. And he takes great joy in preparing everyone for the race with the story of Pheidippides, the Greek runner who runs 40kms from Marathon to Athens to give news of victory in the Battle of Marathon - only to die upon arriving. Thanks Deeks!

Running 42kms is daunting. Never more than when you are standing at the starting line (ok, maybe when you pay the entry fee!). The road is all in front of you. It's a great metaphor for achieving any goal in life. And it's how I look at business and life now.

Bang! The gun goes off and we're away. The excitement is like nothing else. It feels like the pace is on straight away and so many start off quicker than they should. I stuck to my pace which mirrored my goal time of 3 hours 30 minutes. Ambitious for first marathon maybe, but the thought of being out there close to 4 hours was really painful so that's basically how I came up with the goal time.

The first half is meant to be as easy as possible. Comfortable is probably a good word for experienced runners, but to a newbie marathon runner, the thoughts, doubts and "what-if's" flutter in and out of your mind. Staying present in the moment is about the best thing you can do.

I remember the southern most turning point. It's at around the 15km mark and you turn and head long, straight and flat along the virtual length of the Gold Coast another 21km's or so before turning back to head for home.

The course is beautiful. Long stretches of beach on your left for the first half. On your right for the second half. The weather in July is at its coolest but the sun shines in a way that just makes you feel happy. How blissful to be 25kms into a gruelling adventure and suddenly your mind just stops to be grateful - to appreciate beauty. But it doesn't last for long.

Your legs get heavier with every step in a marathon. It's not like riding a bike where you can roll for a bit but continue to keep moving forward. In a marathon, you have to take every step. If you stop, progress stops.

The 30km mark is where things get hard. You hear Marathon enthusiasts talk about "hitting the wall". It seems to happen around here because humans by nature can only store enough glycogen in their cells to provide energy for 2 hours before depletion takes over and the body is forced to slow. Depending on how you've fuelled throughout the race can seriously determine how you feel once you go past the 2 hour mark. Get it right, and you can almost go all day. Get it wrong, and you might be the one passing out head first into the pavement.

Hitting the wall is as much mental for a newbie. It's physical for sure, but if you expect to hit the wall, you probably will. Our mind is powerful. And as a first time marathon runner I knew this moment was coming.

The 32km mark was hurting me. I knew I had 10km in me. I've ran 10km so many times I've lost count. But running 10km when you feel like hell is something else. It was all mental now. One foot in front of the other.

The last 10kms of a marathon is the like the half way point. Like so many goals in life, you start thinking about how far you've come. How much you've got to lose by not finishing. But then you look around and see the support. Strangers you don't even know cheering you on. It's so personal. They look at your face. Sometimes you smile. Sometimes your grimace garners more empathy and support. Either way, you are never alone.

At the centre of a world of hurt, there are people watching on hoping you make it. Encouraging you. It may not be the people closest to you. It doesn't matter. You feel their energy. You are lifted to try harder, keep pushing.

As humans we are so lucky to be gifted with feelings. Emotions that make us do things we wouldn't even think of doing if we were simpler beings.

Seeing a sign with a "40km" on it was a sense of achievement for me. I knew I was going to make it. The crowds that line the Gold Coast highway for the last 2kms of the marathon is something special. It buzzes with electricity. You feel that more than your own legs in the last kilometres.

I crossed the finish line in 3 hours 35 minutes. It was a mixed bag of relief, satisfaction, happiness and exhaustion. And it was beautiful.

Ever since completing my first marathon, I have a bigger belief in myself. That marathon was not my last. I have since ran over 20 of them - including multiple 50km UltraMarathons and even a 100km Ultra through tough mountains (another story!).

I now believe and recommend that everyone run a Marathon. It's not about the running - it's about the person you become in the process.

"Once your mind is expanded by an idea, it will never return to its
original dimension." - Oliver Wendall Holmes

Gold Shoes

Some people start out with such certainty that they never
looked like failing. The absolute congruency that comes with vividly
imagining yourself achieving your goals, is one of the most powerful
things you can practice.

Olympic legend Michael Johnson who won gold medals in
both the 200 metre and 400 metre events in the Atlanta Olympics
knew the power of this. He could see it in his mind so clearly that he
invested more than 2 years lobbying the Olympic Committee to alter
the schedule just to give him a chance. When that failed, he used
track meets across Europe leading up to the 1996 Olympics as a
proving ground to encourage the Olympic Committee to change the
schedule to allow sufficient recovery time for him to prepare for each
race. To add even more pressure, Michael Johnson walked out onto
the track in 1996 at the Olympic Games in a pair of *gold shoes*.
How's that for single minded focus!

Michael Johnson's victories in the 200m and 400m had
never been done before in Olympic history. He went on to become
the first human to successfully defend the 400m title with a Gold
medal at the Sydney Olympics in 2000. He broke 44 seconds for the
400 metres an incredible 22 times, more than twice as many times as
any other athlete. Gold shoes!

The subconscious is a power that fills every cell and space in
this universe. Your natural birthright allows you to access this power
with or without your conscious awareness. Lack of awareness to the
proper use of this power is the ignorance we must all overcome to
enjoy this abundant birthright we each possess. It is a simple
substance that requires no force to exercise. It will deliver exactly

what you give it. The thoughts you permit to exist in your mind create the reality in which you live.

Understanding and application of these Universal Laws will give you anything you can hold in your mind. You already possess all the potential, talents and abilities you will ever need. There is nothing on this earth that can stop you from thinking what you want to think. Knowing and believing this means you see the truth. Even if you don't see it now... you will.

Points To Remember on the Mind:

1. Everything begins with thought.

2. Become childlike and learn to expand your *Circle of Comfort.*

3. What you accept as true in the conscious mind is automatically accepted in the subconscious mind.

4. Your body will produce results that are consistent with conditioning of your subconscious.

5. For the subconscious to be conditioned it requires emotion and/or repetition in order for an idea to pass from the conscious to the subconscious.

6. To successfully program your subconscious, keep your mind ON what you want and keep it OFF what you don't want.

7. The conscious mind has the ability to accept or reject thoughts and ideas whilst the subconscious does not.

8. The subconscious is reactive and works 24/7.

9. The subconscious cannot tell the difference between something that is vividly imagined or real.

CHAPTER 2

Responsibility

"You cannot build a life full of dreams on a foundation of excuses." -
Scott Groves

The Sydney Tower looms large over the city of Sydney on the east-coast of Australia. This enormous structure stands an impressive 305 metres above street level and 235 metres above sea level. It gives visitors a maximum visibility of around 82 kilometres. It has 56 cables that are used to stabilise the tower. If these 56 strands of cable were laid end to end they would stretch from Sydney to New Zealand.

The design of this tower makes it capable of withstanding extreme wind conditions and earthquakes. The foundation and support structure is to say the least solid. Apparently experts in construction can walk up to a hole in the ground where a tower of this sort is to be built and tell you just how high it can go.

Isn't it interesting to note that just by looking at the foundation, someone can predict the height in which one will rise?

And so it is with human achievement.

The foundation to all success must be strong and deep in order for you to rise to great heights. There is not one person on this earth who has risen to such heights and remained there without this foundation. Those that have rose, only to find themselves crashing to the ground some years later can find the source of their collapse in the foundations upon which they built. Responsibility is the foundation upon which all success is built. You cannot build a life full of dreams on a foundation of excuses.

The Enemy of Responsibility is B.E.D.

The victims of this world are people who spend their lives in *BED*. This stands for Blame, Excuses and Denial. I choose not to spend too much time and paper going over these three qualities - if you can call them qualities. I mention them only to serve as a warning sign of what to avoid. Blaming, making excuses and denial are the opposite of responsibility. They are core characteristics of someone who gives their control to others and to the circumstances of life.

When I think of someone who spends their life in *BED*, I think of someone who is missing a tremendous portion of their life. It is a habit of thinking that is rooted in reacting to whatever life hands them. Like a cork in the ocean that is tossed at the mercy of the tides and currents of life. Eventually becoming water logged to where it will sink to rock bottom. Remember the lesson of the cork and let it remind you of the dangers of reacting to circumstances.

Habits

It is important to recognise here that many of our responses to situations are being played out without any conscious thought. To put it another way we are victims of our own habits.

> *"Bad habits are like a comfortable bed, easy to get into but hard to get out of."*

In order to free yourself from the habits that are holding you back you must engage in rigorous self-analysis and ongoing personal development. It is the foundation to all success. If you are not achieving the sort of results you would like then there really is only one place to look, and that place is in the mirror.

As time goes by and you actively pursue the achievement of your goals you will uncover further habits that may need attention. The good news is that we each have successful habits along with our failure habits. The key to real quality of life is to increase the amount of good habits we have and reduce the number of bad habits.

Responsibility is a good habit to develop whilst reacting to circumstances and other people leaves us at the mercy of our bad habits. Responsibility is the common characteristic amongst all successful individuals regardless of their chosen endeavour. You can always tell how high one will rise by the amount of responsibility they are willing to build as their foundation. This attitude of "*I'm in charge*" is the core characteristic with all who have achieved anything meaningful and worthwhile.

These are the sort of people worth studying. I don't think anyone can live long enough to learn it all themselves. This is why I continue to spend a tremendous portion of my time reading and searching the works of some of the greatest minds to walk this earth. Their stories are fascinating. Some of their wisdom has been passed down in the most direct and easy to understand terms. Whilst some of their teachings have been left to interpret from the magic of words they have left behind. The responsibility we all have is to do what we can with what we've got. Jim Rohn said, "If you wish to become successful, study success." It is our personal responsibility to ensure the work of these great men does not drift into the ocean of ignorance where one's life can be doomed to flow with the tides of mediocrity. We are all born into greatness.

Responsibility gives us the power to access this greatness. It gives us control. Responsibility is the ability to respond to the tides of life by putting your rudder in the water and giving your life the direction to arrive at your own Promised Land. The candle of life only burns for so long before many wake to the crashing waves of '*Someday Isle*'. Someday I'll begin that savings account. Someday

I'll take you on that holiday. We should be careful because that someday may never come.

Responsibility is the starting point to all effective accomplishments. In this chapter I will give you some tools that you will need to apply to begin to lay this solid foundation. Whilst there is much I can share with you there is one thing that I cannot do. I cannot walk through the door of opportunity for you. This is your life. What you do with it is your responsibility. It is not a responsibility I would recommend taking lightly when so much is at stake. I hope the seriousness of these words comes across the page to you. I have seen too many people ruin their lives through the misguided use of this principle. Do you know of anyone who has ever wanted more out of life whilst simultaneously complaining and blaming? If you do, soon you will realise their lack of progress is no accident. You can only ever be effective to the degree that you are prepared to accept the credit and the blame yourself.

When we speak in terms of goal setting you will find that you will only ever be truly effective with your goals to the degree that you accept responsibility for your life and the results you get. We are effective with our goals to the degree to which we accept responsibility for both the credit and the blame.

Andrew is a sales manager in a large firm. Each day Andrew is given 100 opportunities to respond to different situations. He consistently gives away 30 of these by complaining, denying responsibility and blaming others around the office. Andrew is only about 70% responsible. To put it another way, Andrew is only 70% in control of what's going on. His frustrations and feelings of useless are directed at the salespeople as he is struggling to reach 70% of his goals.

Understanding this basic principle you will see that your success in all areas diminishes each time that you give power away to circumstance. You can only have maximum effectiveness with your goals if you are 100% responsible.

Your success is always in proportion to your level of responsibility. The people of this world who become frustrated and feel powerless need look no further than to the level of responsibility that they are either taking on or forfeiting. To be 100% effective with your goals and your life, practice becoming 100% responsible for the way you respond to the situations and circumstances of life.

Choose Your Response

The word responsibility is often a misinterpreted word used in many cases to scold children for their naturally childish behaviour. Growing up I heard many parents use the *"Don't be so irresponsible"* plea. It is only now in my later years that I have come to the realisation that responsibility is something that is developed, not something that we are born with. We didn't have this faculty that could reason between what we wanted to accept or reject until eight or so years of age. As a parent I believe it is our responsibility to educate our children on the correct use of this ability as they grow. Up until the development of this ability we are responsible *'for'* our children. They can't be blamed for anything since what they have learned, they have learned through us.

After they have begun to develop the ability to accept and reject information we become responsible *'to'* our children instead of *'for'* them. We must slowly hand over the decision making reigns to them so they can learn the difference between responding and reacting - one of life's most important faculties to develop.

The word responsibility is a two-part word. If you break it down it says response-ability. Ultimately it means the *ability to respond*. Isn't this the concept of what our parents were trying to get across to us when they said, *"Don't be so irresponsible"*. It is a way of saying that we don't like the way someone is acting or responding to a set of given circumstances. It may be that we don't like the way someone is playing with another in the sandpit or speaking with someone in the workplace. Regardless of the situation we each have the ability to respond to any type of circumstance in whichever way we choose. Misuse of this ability to respond is a flaw in the makeup of the person who is failing. By reacting they simply forfeit their right to control the way they feel. In doing so, they give up the power that they are meant to develop as they grow into adulthood. The power of choice.

Whenever you witness someone who is always blaming their circumstances or the way someone has treated them you are witnessing someone who is losing control of their life. Every time you give away the ability to control how you respond you incrementally add to your slave mentality. Imprisoned by circumstances which may be beyond your control but they are not beyond your ability to choose how you feel about them. It is in forfeiting our right to choose that we ultimately chain ourselves.

Life would be boring if everything went the way we wanted it to. It would leave no room for the excitement of anticipation, variety and surprise. Thousands of times per day we take in external information from our surroundings and we either choose how we respond to them or react out of our old conditioning. By taking charge of your choices you develop the freedom mentality. You are no longer bound by what happens, but freed by how you respond to what happens.

Have you ever had the experience of someone criticising or abusing you only to step back from the situation and say to yourself, *"I'm not going to let that upset me"?* It was in that moment that you made a decision on how it would affect you. You have probably also had the experience where someone said something to you and you became upset and said, *"You make me so mad!"* In this instance you have given control to someone else over how you feel.

Reading this now you can probably detect how disempowering this kind of response is. You probably know people who have got out of bed in the morning only to find that it's raining outside and they instantly become depressed as though the day is all over before it begins. Once again the right to respond is forfeited to the habit of reaction. I remember an interview with a world ranked mountain biker who would risk life and limb on treacherous downhill terrains who summed up responsibility in one sentence when he said,

"Pain is inevitable, misery is optional."

The "I" Factor

The language responsible people use is very different to the language of those who are irresponsible. The "I" Factor is developed over time by all responsible people. They have developed the ability to use the word "I" where the irresponsible people of this world use words like they, he, she, it and you. Irresponsible people will blame everything except themselves with comments like, *"You make me so angry"*, *"I can't believe they did this to me"*, and *"If she had just did what I said"* and so on.

When sales are down your average salesperson will begin to blame the leads or the area. In sports, the average performer will say that *"It was too windy"* or *"The sun was in my eyes"*. These people are doomed to mediocrity if they fail to develop The "I" Factor.

The high achievers of this world are personally accountable for every outcome. They say things like *"I could improve on that in the future"*, *"This is what I learned from this experience..."*, *"What I'm going to do now is..."*

Responsible people speak from a position of power. They understand that it's not what happens; it's what you do about it. Never give away the ability to improve and grow with a Freudian slip of the tongue. Developing this habit requires eternal vigilance on your part to master the way you communicate with yourself. Once developed you will be free to pursue your dreams safe in the knowledge that nothing will stand in your way, except your own ability to choose your response to any situation.

"If there is no enemy within: the enemy outside will do us no harm." - African proverb

Press Pause

When we receive stimulus from the outside world we have a period of time to decide how to interpret this information. For those people who believe they are impulsive and tend to react quickly and "fly off the handle" they simply need to realise that they can take as long as they like to decide how they will respond.

When the next person cuts you off in traffic you have a decision to make. If you choose to make no decision you will simply play out the old reaction you have stored away. It may be a honk of the horn or an interesting hand gesture amid some colorful language. But if you choose to pause for a moment and think of another way to respond you may find yourself coming up with some totally different feelings to experience as a result of this outside incident.

Imagine this, you see in your rear view mirror a white sedan racing along the highway at around twice the speed limit swerving in and out of traffic, what would your initial reaction be? Most would probably be thinking "What an idiot". As the car approaches and overtakes you, the driver swerves in front almost taking off your front bumper. Your heart races as adrenaline pulses through your veins. Your knuckles now white with tension grip the wheel as you regain your composure. At this point in time what would you be feeling? Terror, anger, nervous, revengeful. As the car pulls away you notice in the back corner of the window a piece of paper that is stuck on his back window that reads: "Wife in Labor, She's Haemorrhaging, Sorry".

How would you feel upon reading this? It changes the way you see the situation doesn't it? Your response would be somewhat different than if you had no idea why this person was driving like that, wouldn't it? The lesson here is that you have the ability to accept or reject any information. If you were to reject the note on the window and think to yourself, *"Well I don't care it's dangerous and he could still kill somebody"* you may still feel negative emotions. If however you think *"I hope everything is okay for them"* you will likely feel more positive emotions.

What you accept and reject will ultimately have very little effect on others but can have a massive effect on the emotions you experience on a daily basis. Self-mastery lies in eliminating the expression of negative emotions so you can empower yourself to achieve the goals and dreams you have thought about your whole life. We would be naive to think that because we begin down the road of self-fulfilment that nothing is ever going to go wrong. The reason for self-mastery through response-ability is because when you begin pursuing a goal that your heart is set on, everything becomes magnified. The driver who cuts you off in traffic will be nothing compared to someone who roadblocks your dreams.

You need to have the ability to handle these inevitable obstacles. It is only through developing this unique ability which is within us all that you can experience the joy of the journey with less stress and less frustrations.

There are enough stories of millionaires who wind up in the cardiac ward at the local hospital through the neglect of this simple discipline. Take your time to master your responses to every situation. Steer clear of the impulsive reactions that lead to despair and unhappiness. Your future depends upon your ability to lay this foundation and maintain it with everything you've got.

Our Own Reflection

Some people have the physical eyesight to see hundreds or even thousands of metres in front of them whilst others can barely see four feet in front of them. It is the same with our insight. We all have a vision of ourselves. The ability to see with the mind is also limited by our own personal limitations.

However these limitations are not in a physical sense. They are developed through the lack of mental use over the years. People who never consider setting and pursuing goals fail to develop the full potential of their most powerful resource. The mind can be likened to a muscle that has either grown with use or atrophied through lack of use. One of the simplest ways to discover how you truly see yourself is to take a good hard look at what it is you are getting back. In high school we used to say, "*What goes around, comes around*". During the years I have spent studying the mind and its wonders I came across the more scientific definition of the *Law of Cause and Effect*. Whatever you choose to call it makes little difference. The point here is that we attract back that which we put out there into the world. Your outer world is a direct reflection of your inner world.

Think of it like a lemon. Inside a lemon is lemon juice. When you squeeze a lemon, putting external pressure on it, what naturally comes out of it? The obvious answer is whatever is inside it. In this case it would be lemon juice. So what about you?

When the external pressures of the world are squeezing you, what comes out? Does anger come out? How about nasty comments to other people? Or do you show compassion and understanding regardless of your own personal circumstances? This *Law of Correspondence* reflects a mirror image of you back to the world. What comes out of you is directly related to what's inside. If you are filled with bitterness then bitterness comes out. If you are filled with a refreshing sweetness then that is what will come out. The way we treat others is a mirror image reflection of us and perhaps the first place we can look to improve ourselves.

"The real test of character is how you treat others when you are faced with the difficulties in your own life."

Your ability to rise above your own challenges and reach down inside yourself to give away the good you have is one of the toughest yet most rewarding things you will ever do. Many people choose to share their own baggage with virtually everyone they come in contact with. They will moan and groan about how life has done them wrong until they've dragged everyone around them to a level where they can feel superior within themselves again. This is the hallmark behaviour of the insecure individual.

When you begin searching for a pity party you will find no shortage of negative people to share in your grief. Misery does love company.

If you really want to find a way to jumpstart yourself on the road to responsibility, ask those you communicate with most if they can tell just by looking at you, whether you are having a bad day? The easier they can see it in your body language, the bigger the challenge is to eliminate the expression of negative emotions.

"Negative circumstances are simply experiences that we have not emotionally mastered yet." - Scott Groves

We are living magnets and sometimes we are not consciously aware of the good we may be repelling. Good friends are worth their weight in gold. Truly successful people do not want to be anywhere near those who hold pity parties and drag the people around them down. Successful people reject those who let the circumstances of life play havoc with their moods. If you really want to enjoy the fruits that this world has to offer then you will need to enlist the help of successful people.

Since like attracts like, the more positive, energetic and fun you are to be around, the more people you will have that will bend over backwards to help you. You will inevitably attract exactly the type of people you deserve to be around.

This *Universal Law of Cause and Effect* is a neutral law like all of the *Universal Laws*. This means they can be used both positively and negatively. If you are miserable and grumpy you will find yourself mixing more regularly with the company of people who are also miserable and grumpy.

Positive successful people have got better things to do and so do you. Stay away from the type of people who can drag you down and you will find the reflection looking back at you in years from now is the one you have created for yourself. It is your personal responsibility and in the years to come you will only have yourself to thank or blame.

How to Apply Response-Ability to Your Life

The next time you are faced with a different set of circumstances ask yourself:

- If I could see this through the eyes of a successful person who has control over their perspective, how would they choose to see it?
- How would they respond to the situation?
- How should I respond?
- If I was to learn from this experience how would I feel about it once the lesson was learned?
- If I could feel these feelings now, what would that feel like?
- If I could find the opportunity to grow from this experience, what could I become?

The Self Image and Goals

I often ask people how much they would like to increase their income by in the next year. Their answers always intrigue me. Think about this for a moment and write down what financial increase you would like this year so we can come back to it later. Do this now!

Although I get a variety of figures there is one thing in common with each answer. Each answer is normally well within what people are actually capable of. Ask yourself, "*Am I capable of earning more than what I wrote down?*" Is it possible?

A goal is usually set without any conscious awareness of our subconscious characteristics. We blurt out a goal that is guided by the subconscious image we have of ourselves. The three basic subconscious levels of identity, values and beliefs need to be introduced to your goals so your potential can be truthfully explored.

There seems to be a direct relationship between the self image and the increase that is believed possible with regards to one's income or anything for that matter. What is it that prevents us from seriously pursuing an increase of 100%, 200% or even a 1000% increase in income in a single year? Many people have done this and much more. The reason is because we base our goals and what we want to achieve largely on our self image. It slows our ability to achieve greatness more than anything else when setting goals.

If we were to release our limiting images and just dream, we would accelerate the rate at which we achieved our goals enormously. It requires zero willpower to change the self image. Many people aren't aware that this is the case. The majority of people believe that it takes incredible willpower to achieve goals. Willpower is for deciding. It has nothing to do with the actions it takes to achieve. Willpower is only required to create an image of who we are and what we believe we are capable of achieving. Listen to the language used by a cancer patient who is determined to beat their circumstances. I *WILL* be free of cancer. I *WILL* live to see my grandchildren grow up.

Making a decision with willpower is like burning the bridges behind us. Once you decide you will never go back.

It is when we have a poor self image that we make decisions that lack commitment. This is when we must overcome enormous resistance in order to achieve our goals. When we begin to understand the difference between setting true goals that have no boundaries, and goals based on low self images we will set ourselves free. Once the shackles of a poor self image are removed we are free to pursue our dreams without limitations, without resistance. It will be like lifting the anchor on yourself so you can sail to the Promised Land and away from the pirates of your mind.

This is an incredibly important point to understand since most of what's written about in this book is based around the correct use of this principle. You base what you think you can achieve on how you see yourself. The larger the vision you have of yourself, the more you expect to achieve and the larger your goals will be. The questions you will be asking yourself as you progress through this book are for the purpose of developing the type of self image that is required for you to go to a higher level. The larger the vision you hold of yourself, the bigger the goal you will entertain.

Our Goals Reveal Us to Ourselves

> *"You will not seriously want something that you can't achieve." - Bob Proctor*

The fact is that your **'want'** is simply a reflection of something that you are capable of achieving. It is your inner core that delivers the idea to you and it is your responsibility to act on that idea. You are what this world has chosen to channel this idea through. Accept that which is given to you. It was Adlerian Psychotherapist Alfred Adler who said, *"I am grateful to the idea that has used me"*.

We need to understand that life is not a trickster. This universe does not provide people with the ability to desire without complimenting them with the talents and abilities to fulfill those desires. Our subconscious is always trying to become whole. It is always searching for ways in which to become complete and it does so by providing you with desire. It is your personal responsibility to listen to your inner desires and move yourself in the direction of your potential. If you fail to act on this desire it will forever remain in the back of your mind as unfinished business.

By setting and pursuing goals you will be emotionally and spiritually in harmony with your core being. If you have ever had the experience of working in a job that you didn't like you would know what I mean by lack of harmony. We meander through the day thinking about what we really wanted, and emotionally and physically we become drained and unhappy. The reverse of this is pure freedom.

Responsibility gives you the feeling of control. If you have never set goals before now, doing so with responsibility as your ally will help you discover yourself for the first time. You will never discover who you really are or what you are really capable of without setting goals and stretching yourself to achieve them. You are more in control than you realise.

How Fear Reacts

You will be confronted by your own limitations at some stage during your stretch to reach your goals. Outside of your sphere of control lies what most people call fears. As part of my research I was amazed to discover that in America today there are over 700 phobias listed. These are not even the most common fears that we generally refer to, but *full blown phobias*. The misuse of the imagination can be disastrous so let's explore fear from a different point of view.

What I have come to learn about fears is that they are more cowardice than we are. If we just stand up to them they shrink like a balloon having the air let out of it. It's like a see saw battle that goes on where both you and the fear itself are afraid. The fear however has no power. It cannot stand up and become stronger so it relies on you to cower away so it can continue to dominate. The day you stand up to it, it has no other choice but to move aside as it realises that it has no place with you anymore.

"Fear will only ever remain where it is given permission to live." -
Scott Groves

Fear is like a bad tenant that you won't kick out. Eventually the situation gets to the point where you either kick them out or they will bring the house down. When you confront a fear with confidence and boldness it will simply move on. Fear offers no objections and no resistance when you are serious. It knows its time has come.

Next time you are faced with your own fears I want you to see how this approach works. I have come to enjoy watching how fear reacts when I walk towards it. Have you ever tried walking towards your own fear just to see how it reacts? Your heart will be racing with a surge of life flowing through your veins but with each step in the direction of your dreams comes a confidence that is built in no other way. Overcoming a preconditioned fear is mind expanding. We get a different perspective on things once we have walked past the point of no return. We become free.

Pretend you are a fly on the wall as you watch how you handle your own fear. Become the outsider looking in. And rather than becoming emotionally involved in your fear, just observe. Observe what is happening on the outside. Look at the way your posture reacts. Then observe what happens on the inside. Listen to the emotions like an interested counsellor might listen to your tale. As your awareness of the situation begins to heighten you can then bring yourself back and start to take charge of the situation. If you must fail at anything in life, fail to react. Take personal responsibility over your posture and physiology. Grab the reigns of control and summon the emotions of courage, certainty and choice. Put some passion into your decision to move forward in the face of danger. Fear doesn't have teeth. As an onlooker you can do this quite easily. Sometimes we are too close to our own situations to realise that we are caught in our own web. Become a fly on the wall and with non-judgement you will walk right over the top of your fear.

Monster Under the Bed

I had an experience as a young boy of around 8 years. I was scared of the monster that was under my bed. I don't know if you had one of these when you were growing up.

My room was dark and I was stricken with fear every night for a couple of months. I lay there and wouldn't call out to Mum and Dad in case I disturbed this monster of the dark. He hid behind a decorative blue curtain that covered the area between my mattress and the floor. My bed was situated on the far side of the room. In order to get to the light switch or escape into the hallway I had to walk across the entire width of the room. There I stayed confined to my bed by my own mental prison unable to find my way to the freedom I so desperately sought. I never did run away from it just as I didn't confront it. A predicament I'm sure that many could relate to.

One night I finally mustered up enough courage. I was going to stare this hairy beast in its cold, merciless eyes and declare my bedroom my own. Like an adventurer journeying to a new land I would drive my flag of courage into the ground and stake my claim. I slowly pulled back the sheets as I mentally surveyed the distance to the door. I could feel the coldness on my legs as I turned sideways to put my feet on the floor, hoping nothing would grab me. I finally had my feet on the floor. Fear gripped my feet. I would like to say that I walked boldly to that light switch but I didn't. Each step was measured and silent. You could have heard a pin drop. My heart was beating so loud that I thought the neighbours would wake. I finally made it to the door where I turned the light on. The last thing I had to do now was lift the cover that hung between my mattress and the floor. My trembling hand grabbed hold of the blue material and ever so slowly lifted it as I peered underneath. I guess like all fears when you are prepared to stare them in the eye, they disappear. I will never forget the relief I felt when I realised there was no monster. I looked twice under the bed just to make sure. With a couple of nights of checking under my bed my bravery was growing. This experience was so real for me that it took me a few nights to really believe that nothing was there.

The lesson I learned was this...

Fear only has the power we give it. Failure to confront fear only makes it worse. I remind myself of this if I let fears of rejection or fears of failure creep in under my bed. I know that there are some fears we must face more than once before they are banished for good. But when you turn on the lights the monsters are gone.

"There is not enough darkness in the world to extinguish the light of one small candle." - Spanish Proverb

With just a little bit of bravery we can overcome the fears that keep us in the dark. Once you make a decision to live your dreams you will find the courage you need to overcome what your mind has fictitiously created. Your fears may be powerful but remember you are only born with one.

The most powerful way to discover just how much the subconscious fears are holding you back is to ask yourself, "If I was absolutely guaranteed of success, what would I be doing differently, that I am not doing right now?" If the answer to this is something that you are not currently doing then I would suggest that the only reason you are not doing it, is because of some sort of fear. Perhaps the fear of failure. Perhaps something else. Either way it is your responsibility to overcome your fears. No one can do it for you.

The Mental Hypochondriac

Have you ever read an article about a disorder or complaint like chronic fatigue? It gives you all of the symptoms like tiredness, lack of concentration, muscle aches and pains and occasional headaches. By the end of the article you feel like you've got it?

Fears are much like this also. Based on what we have learned so far you will remember that we get what we focus on. What would happen if you were to spend all of your thinking about how to overcome your fears? They would inevitably get worse because the *Law of Substitution* says that *"the conscious mind can only hold one thought at a time"*. We can and should be replacing our fear thoughts with thoughts of strength, courage and bravery. Begin to focus on the characteristics that you consistently want to use in all areas of our life. A mind spent dwelling on fear is a subconscious mind absorbing fear.

When I first got into sales I had a meeting with the General Manager. A man named Mark Neil who asked me if I had ever done any selling before. My answer was "no". It wasn't that I hadn't. I just believed that I hadn't. The fact was that I had built my own tennis coaching business from the age of seventeen. From zero to a hundreds of pupils per eight week term over the eight years involved everything to do with selling. I was out there approaching schools, writing my own ads, giving away group lessons to attract new customers, phoning people to book them in and re-signing them term after term. How naive I was to think I wasn't selling.

It wasn't until I *"officially"* started a career in direct sales that I began reading books specific to selling that taught me things like *'how to overcome rejection'*. I read so much on the subject that I began to develop the fear. Here I was from a young age afraid of nothing, totally ignorant to what salespeople are supposed to go through whilst I built a successful tennis coaching business. I shifted from sales books to books on how to overcome fears. I became the analytical expert on the subject and discovered that we can become our own mental hypochondriac. Throughout my coaching and training years I began to reflect on the people that were paralysed by fear and those who took massive action. I found that their mental focus played a major part in the amount of fear they experienced.

Since we are not born with fears of rejection and fears of failure we must shift our mental focus. Time spent reading about the symptoms is time spent developing them. If you want symptoms of fear then read and think about them all day long. If you want symptoms of success then spend all day thinking about confidence, decisiveness, courage, solutions and excitement until your wallet bursts.

I have already wasted too much paper talking about fear so I hope the lesson is conveyed well so I never have to write about it again. Fear is a fruitless focus that makes mental hypochondriacs of us all. It is a coward that will shrink from your life the day you refuse to feed it.

Unleash Your Identity - the Foundation to Your Dreams

Put your goals and what you want to achieve out of your mind for the moment. We have discussed how our goals are largely based on what it is we see ourselves capable of achieving. I want you to build the foundation upon which your goals should really be set.

I am going to suggest that you write down a list of the positive characteristics and qualities that you possess. Start off the sentences with the words I am...

Keep writing past the point of twenty qualities so that your list looks something like this;

- I am great with people
- I am talented at...
- I am honest
- I am ethical
- I am a confident person
- I am outgoing

- I am...

Get the idea? Do this NOW!

Remember that the more successful you are, the faster you will act on the information presented before you.

If you haven't written your list out please do so now so you get the impact of this. I have a point to make here so go ahead and do this now if you want to experience this impact.

Look at your list of qualities and ask yourself, *"If someone possessed all of these qualities and characteristics, what would they be capable of?"* Really look at your list for a moment, what could this person, with all of these characteristics do? In the seminars I've ran, around 98% of the audience will answer - *"ANYTHING!"*.

The truth is that a person with all of these attributes *would* be capable of anything.

Now look at your list again and come to the realisation that this person is YOU.

Once you have began to identify with this person I want you to look at the amount of income increase you wrote down before. As you look at it you will begin to realise just how achievable this figure really is.

You begin to see yourself in a whole new light as you bring to your conscious awareness a part of you that quite often gets taken for granted. By focusing on these qualities and characteristics you begin to intensify their power through the *Law of Substitution*. By focusing on your positive attributes, your mind is not distracted by circumstances. This causes any negative qualities you have to dissipate through the lack of attention they are given. Your actions begin to fit a pattern based on your developing identity that is being reinforced through your new focus.

This focus will allow you to unleash your identity and you can begin to build a foundation of goals based on a person with all of the qualities and characteristics that you possess. You begin by bringing a part of you that is furthest from conscious awareness to the floor through mastering the art of responsibility. You choose to focus on your characteristics that will take you to the achievement of your goals. By focusing on them you set the picture more firmly in your mind. As you do this your vision of what you are really capable of begins to grow. Soon you are deciding to go for goals that five years ago you would have never dreamed possible.

You have unleashed your identity and with it, anything becomes possible.

Points to Remember on Responsibility

1. We may not be responsible for everything in our subconscious but we are responsible for what is allowed to stay in there. If you have weeds pull them out!

2. You cannot control circumstances but you do control how you respond to them.

3. The *Greatest Power* you have is the *Power of Choice*.

4. The way you feel about yourself is in direct proportion to your focus. As you focus on the things you can control you raise your self-esteem and positive feelings about yourself.

5. It's not what happens, it's what you do about it.

6. To be 100% effective with your goals and your life you must become 100% responsible for every situation or circumstance.

7. Your success will be in direct proportion to the foundation of success you build through your ability to respond.

8. People set goals based on the picture they have of themselves.

9. Unleash your identity so you can accurately see the possibilities based on the qualities and characteristics you possess.

10. Your desire to achieve something is your potential beginning to express itself. Recognise desire for what it is.

CHAPTER 3

Values

Values are like the glue that makes you stick to your goals. They are cornerstone to commitment. Values create congruency with your goals. The ultimate time management tool that could save you countless wasted years spent chasing your tail on goals that don't inspire you. Most people don't have the level of conscious awareness that is required to make sure they stick to what it is they are aiming for. Values operate on a deep subconscious level. They are further from our conscious awareness than our beliefs.

Why are they so critical?

Let me answer this by asking you a question, have you ever had the experience of setting upon a goal only to find that a month or two later you hadn't really done much about it? Perhaps you lost your motivation for it? If you are like me you surely have done this at least once in your life, maybe even more. It may have been something that really excited you and you just failed to follow through on it for some unknown reason. Well I can tell you that the unknown reason is foreign no more. The biggest reason you, me and the rest of the world has failed to follow through on one or more of our goals in the past was because our goals were not in harmony with our highest values.

Peace of Mind

A vital step in goal setting is determining your values. When your goals are in line or congruent with your values, you will have 'Peace of Mind'. Peace of mind is part of the journey. People often believe that peace of mind is only achieved when they achieve their respective goals. I was once a victim of this type of thinking and it caused me enormous frustration and inner turmoil. The anticipation of finally achieving a major goal can become empty if we do not enjoy the time we spend in achieving it.

It took me some time to learn two very important distinctions with regards to peace of mind and satisfaction. I learned that peace of mind was achieved when I was chasing something that was worthwhile and meaningful to me, a goal that I truly valued. Satisfaction was the joy of having arrived at the final destination. To experience a life of fulfilment means to live and act consistently with your highest values. This is where you'll find peace of mind. Peace of mind is determined by how you journey toward your destination.

You get given a one way ticket in this life. Each day a portion of its trip is used and no refund will ever be given. You owe it to yourself to pursue what it is that truly makes you happy. Pursue that which gives you the most enjoyment. Take careers as an example, many people refuse to base their careers around the things that they really love to do because they are concerned that doing it on a daily basis might mean that it loses some of its shine. Just because it becomes your career doesn't have to mean the monotony of it will cause you to dislike it. To me this doesn't seem like a valid reason not to do what you love for a living. Let's take an analytical approach to this for a moment and then I will explain what this has to do with goal setting.

Most people work eight hours a day, forty eight weeks of the year for the best part of forty years. That's around 76,800 hours of work. A fairly large chunk of your life, I think you would agree. If even two of those eight hours was consumed doing things that seemed a bit mundane and the other six hours was spent doing what you love, wouldn't it be better than spending 76,800 hours doing something that you didn't like.

I share the same belief as that of Les Brown when he said that, "*I don't believe man was born to work for a living; I believe he was born to make what he lives for, his work*".

A man in one of our seminars once described this approach as the greatest time management lesson he ever learned. Instead of trying to scrounge twenty minutes a day here and there he said, "*This has probably saved me decades of my life*". And it makes sense as to why. If you start out with each of your goals closely aligned to the most important things in your life then you will always be fulfilled knowing you are working on the things that bring you the most joy.

What were you put on this earth to achieve? What is it you value most in your life? Values are essentially things, feelings and characteristics that are important to you. Many of your values will satisfy your basic human needs. They have an effect on how you feel. If your actions are not in harmony with what you value then you begin to feel *'Out of Sync'*. When your actions are in harmony with your values then you will feel fulfilment and peace of mind. If you have ever had someone ask you to do something that was against what was important to you then you would understand what I mean by *'Out of Sync'*.

Actions and Decisions

> **All of our actions and decisions are based**
> **upon what we value and believe.**

Mary is given a good career opportunity that requires moving interstate. However, Mary is faced with a dilemma because her mother who lives near her is sick. Mary's mother is trying to convince her to go as there is little that can be done to help her other than the comforting conversations they share.

The decision that Mary makes about whether to move and take the opportunity or stay and take care of her mother will be eventually determined by her values. If she values family or more specifically the special bond with her mother, more than her career then she will stay. If she values her career, more than her mother, she will go.

Upon reading this simple example you may have decided what you would do in this situation. Other people may take longer as they weigh up what's most important to them. There is nothing right or wrong about a person's set of values. Understanding how values are directing one another's behaviour is what gives us understanding with one another. Understanding our own values is what gives us understanding with ourselves.

The clarity that comes from gaining a clear perspective on what it is you value most is like turning on the lights after having lived in the dark your entire life. For some people that is literally how it feels. Do values change? Of course they do. I had a unique experience where I became terribly run down with my health due to glandular fever. I spent almost three months virtually bed ridden, exhausted day in and day out. It pushed my relationship to the very brink. I wasn't seeing my friends at all.

For almost a year I suffered on and off with Chronic Fatigue. I had bouts of sweating where I would wake up three to four times a night to change my clothes and the towels I was laying on to stop the sheets from getting saturated. Just when I thought it couldn't get any worse I had a scare with my health that I just didn't see coming. I had returned to work but I still didn't have the same spark and zest for life that I was used to. As a professional tennis player and coach I was a person used to boundless energy. My body now felt like it should have belonged to someone else. Anyone but me.

I went to the doctors for a liver function test where they take a sample of blood to determine the enzyme levels in the bloodstream. It is measured in International Units per Litre (IU/L). The abbreviated name for the most sensitive liver reading is ALT. The normal range is to vary somewhere between 0-40. Some doctors believe that anything under 50 is still okay. My doctor explained to me that a reading of 90 is dangerous as the risk of becoming jaundice and hospitalisation increases the higher the reading goes. A few days later I received the results. My liver reading was 376. My body was instantly flooded with uncertainty. I kept thinking, "*What does this mean?*" I was scared. I went home and the minute I walked in the door, I began to cry. I knew I needed dramatic change and I needed it fast. I have always been fit and healthy and eaten well, but it was time to go to another level. I was tired, scared and I'd had enough. The doctor insisted on giving it a label. A liver reading like this meant to him that I had hepatitis. I rejected that thought instantly from my mind and saw it only as a challenge to return to normal. I knew the liver had the ability to regenerate so that's all I saw.

I stopped work and took more time off. I began seeking help, exercising with light walks every morning. A fortnight later I went back for another test and this time my reading had increased to 480. I couldn't believe it. I was planting the right seeds and honestly expected a more positive result. What I wasn't doing was paying attention to the *Law of Gender* that says, "*Everything has a gestation period*". My impatience made me think the seeds I was planting would blossom overnight. Life doesn't work like that. This time I responded differently. I got mad.

I immediately set a goal - "*Liver readings back to safe level of 80 or under by October 15th*". I changed my diet and I leaned up 7 kilograms that I didn't think I even had there to lose. My energy was slowly increasing and I was starting to look like an athlete again. Two and a half weeks later I went back for a third liver function test. The girls at the blood bank now knew me by name. The next day I went to get my results and my ALT liver reading had dropped to 80. The doctor was so amazed that he even asked me how I did it. I had relief at last. I was able to return to work and begin my life again.

I learned the hard way that if we don't truly value our health then our personal world can literally fall apart. This once again proved to me that unless we place a high value on the things that are most important to us then our actions won't change. And if our actions don't change, then nothing will.

The day I got clear on what was important to me with my health is the day that everything began to change. My health had affected everything. Energy, relationships, friends, working life - the lot! And because I valued *feeling good*, *friendships*, *contributing* is so important to me, along with the *peace* I get from being *healthy*, (5 values in that one sentence) it was enough importance for my actions to change. I once again felt the congruency that came from working hard on the things that I valued.

As you clarify your values you will begin to experience the same. Getting clear on what's most important to you in your life is the starting point to dramatic change. Change that will produce results so extraordinary that people will ask you, "*How did you do it?*"

Evolution

Many people have experienced intense emotional events in their lives to find a shift taken place within them. It is part of the evolution we go through as we age. These following examples are generalisations but they are used to illustrate a point. In the teenage years we value fun. In our twenty and thirties we value our careers. In out thirties and into our forties relationships are valued a lot more. People in their sixties tend to value family more. People in their seventies tend to value their independence. Yes there are always exceptions to these generalisations.

People naturally evolve differently from one another. We are all unique and we each encounter different experiences from which we grow. I know twenty-year olds that still live in this "fun only" mentality. Financial security isn't valued anywhere near as much as having fun and as a result they spend their entire pay as soon as they get it. They live for the now with little thought for their financial future.

Over time there may be a stage in life where they miss out on some 'major fun' due to the lack of funds and their financial values may turn. Either way, the point is that their current set of values is determining their behaviours and the results they are getting.

Having worked closely with the elderly I know the importance they place on their quality of life and their independence. If you strip away their independence to the point where they find themselves faced with the harsh reality of a nursing home you often see a value held very high.

For those that value life over and above independence to the point where it is little contest, they find they can move quite easily into the homes of care without the mental anguish.

For those who really value their independence, the decision to even consider a nursing home is a painful experience.

Now that you understand the importance of values and how they dictate the way we make decisions and how we feel about them, we need to determine where your values are now. By doing this you can then build your goals around the things that are most important to you in your life.

Your Core Values

How do you go about determining what it is you value? First make a list of everything that is important to you. You can do a general list or one that is specific to areas of your life. For example you have a home life, a family life, personal life, a career and your health. In each of these areas you value different things. The more often you are faced with difficult decisions in that area of your life, the clearer you will be about what you value. This is the reason why some people walk the talk at the office and fail in the home. Some people's lives evolve around making the important decisions at the office and shun them when they are home.

Values need to be the rocks upon which you can stand when you need them. There comes a point in life where you need to take this stand with yourself. It is from there that you will move forward. There can be no wishy-washy thinking or fluffy decision making on the road to your dreams. When you come to a fork in the road you need to decide. Even if you know what lies on the roads ahead, you must choose which road you want to travel. People who achieve incredible results in such short periods of time do so because of their ability to choose wisely and without lengthy delays. Their unshakable poise and clarity about what's important to them means that every decision moves them towards their goals like a bullet.

Begin by writing down a list of all the things you value. Below I have provided you with some that you may want to include on your list. Take plenty of time collating your list, because once we have collated we are going to start defining them. I would recommend a good hour or two over a couple of days putting your list together. Think about all of the things that you really value in life. Upon completion of your list you will then want to take as much time as necessary for defining them following the guidelines I have laid out for you ahead. This should be something that you do in solitude. It is best done in quiet. You may prefer the beach or a forest. Somewhere tranquil is always a great way to get in touch with your inner most self. The office is definitely not the right place. The home is also questionable if you risk being disturbed.

There is no question that discovering your inner most values is a very necessary part of this process. Once completed it will only require some revision from time to time so see if they are still congruent with how you feel. The effort that you make now will set you up for the future. The clarity that comes with defining your values will serve to give you greater vision for your future and the goals you will achieve.

Remember there is no right or wrong so just be true to yourself. If it only took eight hours to change your life for the better forever, would you do it? It may not even take that long. Remember it is not a race and we are not out to prove how quickly we can do them. Get your values system defined in a way that they feel right for you.

If you can find it within yourself to stop now and complete this exercise then nothing will stop you.

It only gets easier from this point on. So go ahead and challenge yourself. There are no prizes for finishing the book first, but for completing the exercises to the best of your ability there are so many rewarding things you will experience and have as a result that together we could fill another book. Take the time right now. I promise that you will never be the same again from this point on.

To help you on your way I have provided a list of values that you can tick or delete as they apply to you.

List Them
List the most important things to you in your life now!
Tick all the values below that you personally value.

Health   Time
Integrity   Love

Career	Adventure
Family	Passion
Spiritual	Peace of Mind
Personal Freedom	Growth
Fun	Happiness
Contribution	Financial Independence
Friends	Balance
Loyalty	Solitude
Ideas	Learning

Add the extra values that you have thought of here.

-
-
-
-
-
-
-
-
-
-
-
-
-
-

Values - Means to an End

Now that you have listed your values I want you to take a good hard look at them. Before we get on to placing them in an order of priority we need to understand what it is that people really value. There are really two types of values and when listing values like you just have, you may find that you wrote down what I like to call *"Means Values"*. *Means Values* are generally things, people or places. For example, marriage is not really a value. Marriage means something to us. To dig a little deeper into what marriage means is the real value or what I like to call *"End Values"*.

End Values are generally feelings or qualities in people (characteristics) that we value. If you are married or in a relationship, ask yourself, *"What does this relationship mean to me?"* If marriage means feelings of belonging and love to you then you have identified the End Values. The characteristics of your partner that you value might be loyalty, commitment and sharing.

Means and *End Values* are important because it gives you greater clarity when you come to prioritise what is most important in your life. Trying to prioritise marriage is difficult without the meaning because it is just a word on a piece of paper. But when you add the specifics of what a marriage means to you then you have a basis on which you can prioritise with some accuracy.

Remember that the subconscious is driven by what it is that you value and believe. Most of all it is driven by emotions. The *End Values* are the emotional values that carry the power of influence over our behaviour.

To put this in perspective with our subconscious model shows that our *End Values* are on a deeper subconscious level than our *Means Values*. You can always tell how true this is by how easy it is to answer. *Means Values* are much easier to recognise than the *End Values* because they are closer to your conscious awareness.

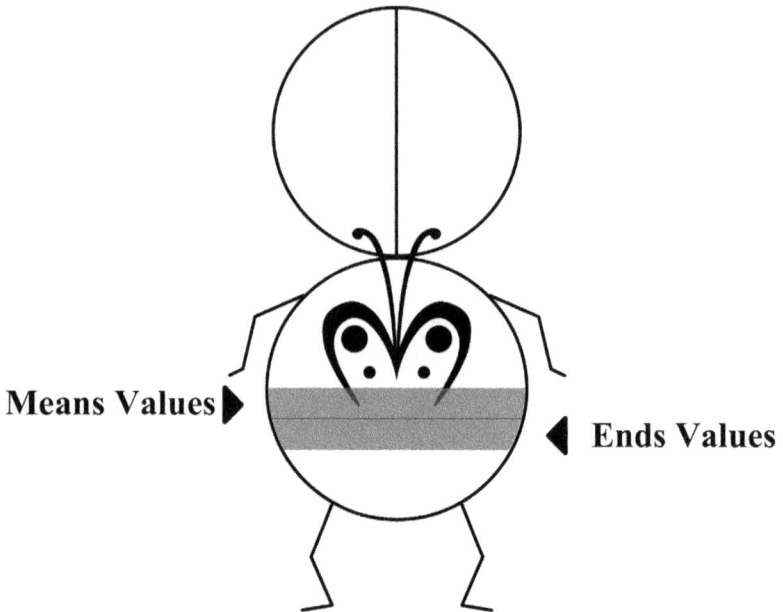

Means Values ▶   ◀ **Ends Values**

Define Your Values

The next step in this value session is to write a short definition for each value. You might be wondering why?

The purpose of the definition is because two people can interpret a word or value on its own in two different ways. If you have ever seen two people arguing over the same thing where they both seem to be agreeing you will know what I am talking about. It is the meaning that we give to things that creates the confusion. These meanings create individual, personal connotations that we each have for different words, principles and values in our society. Over time we can become fuzzy about what it is our own values mean to us. In order to give clarity it is best to define our values. We need to do this in a measurable way. Emotions, much like our *End Values,* can be difficult to measure.

Let's take honesty as an example. Even in different circumstances some people change the rules to suit themselves. One definition might be, "*Be totally open and honest even if it means hurting someone's feelings*". In a different situation it might be, "*Well if they don't ask I won't tell them because I don't want to hurt their feelings*". In each case this person would have justified to themselves that they were honest and upheld their value system.

A person who has a clear definition must act in a certain way regardless. It forces them to live by their rules. There can be no ducking and weaving for the person with a clear set of values. They take what they have to take on the chin and get on with life. A person who values peace of mind might define it as, "*that feeling of serenity, and tranquillity that comes from doing the right thing by myself and others in all situations*".

Here are 4 questions you can use to define your values -
1.   How will you know when this value is satisfied?
2.   How do you measure it?
3.   What feelings do you associate to this value?
4.   What activities satisfy this value?

Here is an example from my own personal list of values and how I defined them. The definitions gave me the clarity I needed to prioritise accurately.

Step #1 List	Step #2 Define	Step #3 Priority
What values are most important to me in my life?	1. How will I know when this value is satisfied? 2. How do I measure it? 3. What feelings do I associate to this value? 4. What activities satisfy this value?	If I had to choose, which would be the most important to me in my life?
Adventure	1. Running in nature or in the rain gives me a sense of adventure. 2. Doing something new and spontaneous (each month) 3. Seeing something "live" - live music, live sport, even a live busker on the street. 4. Travel - day trips, plane	Number 1 priority in this case for me is **LOVE**
Love	1. Uninterrupted family time where we ALL feel the connection and bonds grow. One on ones and total family time together. 2. Dinner at table together with zero technology 3. Eye contact, quality conversations with good listening, hugs that are held. 4. Feelings of belonging, sharing, security, at ease.	Number 2 priority for me in this case would be ADVENTURE

These answers will help to give you clarity when under fire. In pressure situations when you are forced into a corner and a decision has to be made, you can call on your list and definitions for guidance.

Remembering that these are core values that were made in calmness and reflection is very comforting. This list was not made under duress so you know you can trust it when the heat is on.

Prioritise Technique

When it comes time to make a really important decision in your life (like setting a major goal) you will inevitably come back to the thing that you value most. Many people attempt to construct a value system that suits their goals instead of setting goals based on what it is they value.

You will only ever act to satisfy a no.2 value when there are no negative consequences for your no.1 value.

Understanding your priorities allows you to make tough decisions without the fear of remorse. For example, when you have a baby, you naturally begin spending less time with your friends. If spending time with your friends meant interrupting your child's sleep pattern, then you might not do it. As long as there are no negative consequences for your child (and yourselves as parents as a result) then you catch up with your friends. And you can do so without remorse. As children age, this has all gets easier. Understanding this allows parents to continue to live in harmony with their highest values.

Take the necessary time to prioritise your list of *Means* and *End Values* along with your definitions using the following method. Begin by choosing the value that you feel is most important to you. Place this as your No.1 value for the moment while you test it against all others. Let's assume you chose health. Now you must take the time to go through your list and ask yourself this question with every other value.

"If I had to choose between my health and _____ , what would I choose?"

If health remains as the No.1 value then move onto the second most important value. You can probably now see the difficulty of this task for they are not easy questions to answer.

Note: If you get stuck you can do the bottom up technique which involves asking yourself this question.

"If I had to move one value to the bottom of my list which would it be?"

This technique I find has merit but does tend to make people stall on the really important priorities. I like to use extreme examples and mentally play with the situations as though they were real. Extremes cause us to face up to what we value more readily.

You do not have to wait until you think your list is 100% right. Intellectually prioritising on paper will not give you the deep down congruency that comes with living them.

Try Them On

Once you feel you have completed your list in the order you feel most comfortable and empowered by, I want you to take time to wear your values around like you would a new piece of clothing. This is a way of reviewing your order of priorities to make sure that it sits right with you.

Write down your top six to eight values on a card. Carry it around with you and make every decision and action in harmony with your values. You will begin to notice either peace of mind or conflict. Be aware of what it is your feeling. As you wear your values around you will soon discover (within days) whether you have them in the right order or not. Your *Circle of Comfort* will expand as you say "NO" to activities that steal time away from your highest priorities. Give yourself time to adjust before you decide what you're going to live by.

Having a clearly defined and prioritised list of values is invigorating. It is like breathing in fresh mountain air into your lungs. Having clear values lifts the burden of many tough decisions of the future and allows you to live each day as though it were your last. The most important things in your life will always be getting the attention they deserve.

The second reason for trying them on is you don't feel the pressure of having to get them right the first time. Values are a major part of your life. You want to give them time to settle in. You want to be able to go about defining them and prioritising them without the fear of making a mistake. If you had to get them right on paper then it would naturally create unnecessary pressure. And as I said before, it is difficult to intellectually prioritise such an emotional list.

Knowing that you can try them on is like giving yourself a money back guarantee on your values. If you are not 100% satisfied simply return and we will exchange them until you are completely satisfied.

Attract and Repel Values

Values for each area of our lives can be divided into two basic categories. We each have values that we are attracted to and ones that we repel. Any value can fit in either of these categories depending on how it is defined.

For example, commitment is a value that some people are attracted to, whilst some people repel it. The same goes for things like uncertainty or responsibility. Some people hit a wall with responsibility and cease to want to take on any more. Others will take as much as they can get. It all comes down to how your values are shaped for you personally.

Commonly, and I am generalising a little here but commonly people are attracted to things like money, love, family, freedom, health and so on. Values that generally fit the repel category include things like racism, prejudice, injustice, abuse, poverty and so on.

Why are attract and repel values important?

It is important to understand because for some people they may have found that the values (qualities or characteristics) that will get them where they want to go are on the wrong side of the equation.

In order to achieve major goals in life it is important we have commitment and responsibility on the attract side of the equation. Imagine if these were things that you were repelling. The entire foundation to your success would be leaking like a boat with a hole punched through the bottom of it. The chances of keeping your goals afloat would be slim.

However, if you were to balance the equation so to speak, then you would have harmony. All of your actions would naturally flow in the direction of your dreams like a river to the sea.

Financial abundance is best achieved when you are highly attracted to wealth and you highly repel poverty. There is congruency here. If you repelled an abundance of money and also repelled poverty there would be inner turmoil. This inner turmoil creates mixed emotions that will play tug-of-war with your life. Your subconscious will pull you away from poverty when things are tight, then turn around and hold you back when things begin to get too good. I know this sounds crazy on the surface but when you look deep into the thoughts behind it as we will discuss in the chapter on beliefs you will understand how people can do this to themselves.

Understanding these values and their definitions will be the key determinant in you avoiding the following pitfall.

Conflict and Self Sabotage

Conflict and self sabotage occur when there is an inconsistency with our values. It is a feeling you get. This inner turmoil could be likened to a fight between your attract and repel values. For some people this occurs on a major scale. For others it is more subtle and hides itself behind a veil of mini-successes almost teasing us with the vision of a real breakthrough.

Once your values are in alignment there is nothing that will stop you. Every action and decision begins to 'sit right' with you. It develops a gut feeling within you that things are finally on the right track and you are able to move ahead with greater clarity and certainty. The inner civil war of conflict is resolved.

How do you determine whether you might have a conflict of values?

You start by developing your list of repel values. You then compare your list of prioritised repel values with the ones you are attracted to. Then you take a look at your list and look for conflicts. It's that simple.

Without getting into the complexities of the definitions I'll give you a basic example to demonstrate what I mean by conflict.

William (not his real name) is on his third marriage. He blames his first two wives for the demise of the first two marriages.

Going through his list of values it didn't take too long to see it was his conflicting values contributing to the divorces.

William's values were as follows:

Attract Values: Freedom, Family, Love

Repel Values: Commitment, Belonging, Responsibility

Just by looking at William's list you can probably see the conflict amongst some of his values.

William's ultimate value is the feeling of freedom. Whilst he says that family is his no.2 value he simultaneously repels commitment, belonging and responsibility. It would be natural for anyone with a values system structured this way to suffer from inner conflict and confused emotional states. As William began moving closer to becoming a part of a family he would repel the commitment, belonging and responsibilities that go with the territory and pull back in order to maintain his freedom.

In order for William to free himself from his own emotional bungee rope he needs to change the meaning of some of his values so he can achieve some congruency and inner peace.

Ultimate freedom for William was to create a life where he was in charge of his destiny. To experience true freedom and ultimate love now means William is committed to being free enough to express his love. Belonging means he can experience the fullness of love. Responsibility means William is in charge and his true freedom is being exercised daily in his freedom to choose how he feels and not blaming those around him that he loves so dearly.

Once William's associations changed then his whole life changed. It took on new meaning with commitment and belonging switching from feelings that he once repelled to feelings he would enjoy as a result of having a family.

A simple shift in values can literally turn a life around 180 degrees. It forms the underlying reason of importance that goals are aimed at satisfying. True fulfilment and true peace of mind can only come when you are living each day in harmony with what is most important to your core. Bringing your values to your conscious awareness gives clarity and meaning to the goals you are about to set for yourself.

Points to Remember on Values

1. The biggest reason people fail to follow through on their goals is because they are not congruent with their highest values.

2. All of our decisions and actions are based upon what we value and believe.

3. Peace of mind can only be achieved when you are operating in harmony with your highest values.

4. Understanding - Values determine actions, action tell you the values.

5. List your values - The *Means* and the *End*.

6. You will define your values differently to anyone else. It's critical to understand what each value means to you.

7. People who are succeeding make decisions the first time a situation arises in 80% of cases. This is because they are clear on their values where people who are failing are not.

8. Prioritise your values using the means, end and definitions to gauge them by - not just the word.

9. Try them on. You cannot intellectually feel the difference your prioritised values will make to your life. Give them time to settle in.

10. Your *Attract* and *Repel Values* must be in alignment to avoid inner conflict and self-sabotage.

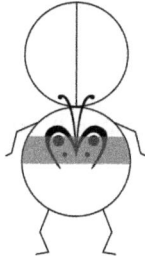

CHAPTER 4

Goals

Before we begin the goal setting process I want to emphasise what this step is actually about. Or more importantly what this step is not about. The act of goal setting is not about timelines, it's not about boundaries or limits and it's not about what society commonly refers to as 'realistic'. Each and every person on this earth is capable of anything that they have a burning desire to achieve.

"With a willing heart, anything becomes possible."

I believe in the potential of people and I am very resistant to those who attempt to put limits on what someone else is capable of. Who are we to say what someone else is capable of. The right of that opinion rests solely with each of us as individuals. When we come to the point of setting our own goals, we must act as our own personal freedom fighters that are fighting for the right to dream.

This section is all about releasing our grip on what's possible or impossible and tapping into our childlike dreams again where we believed we could fly. Since each of us usually base our goals on our self image we must practice the art of doubting our doubts so we can begin to explore what we would really like to be, do and have. We let the subconscious elements that we have discussed so far play a more influential role in our goals. We look at our identity and our values and begin to set goals based on those rather than having no conscious awareness of our subconscious qualities.

What would you do, be or have if you knew you couldn't fail?

Think about that for a moment. Think about the possibilities. We have already determined that with your qualities and characteristics you are capable of anything! Let go of what you have achieved in the past and begin with a clean slate. Set goals based on desires, not the false measuring stick of past achievements. Remind yourself that you are starting with a new set of tools, new knowledge and a new proven method that people are currently using to achieve their goals. So what do you really want in this life?

This chapter is designed to provoke, stimulate, challenge and expand your thinking. It's designed to stretch your thinking in a way that 95% of people never think. You will move beyond the dream stage and journey towards the possibilities that exist within you. Many of us want more out of life and have no idea where to start. Many people see those who are succeeding and become amazed at their outstanding achievements. Let's look at what they do and learn from them.

The beginning is where you will question yourself and your life, the path that all successful people travel. These questions cause you to dream. The vision of this dream that you hold in your mind will translate into a goal and manifest itself into the reality that we each can create for ourselves. There are no secrets to success. Success is predictable. If you want to improve your health, you can. If you want wealth, you can have it. If you want to be happy, you can be. The answers are within you. Sometimes we just need to ask ourselves better questions to find the answers we seek.

Where many people get held up is by trying to find out all of the 'how to's' before they set upon their goal. The bottom line is you will never discover all of the how to's until you begin to pursue your goals. It is really only by doing that you gain the experience necessary to go the distance. There will always be a degree of uncertainty involved. It is one of our human needs. It is important to have uncertainty in its correct proportions because absolute certainty equals absolute boredom. For now you must shift your attention to the life you would like to have. Give in to your noble desires. Following are a few exercises for you to complete. I am often asked how long it takes to complete these exercises and I have always responded with *"Well it depends on the type of life you want to create?"* People are satisfied with different things. If you don't want much then it probably won't take very long. The great Pyramids of Egypt no doubt took longer to build than the weatherboard house I grew up in as a kid. I am also certain that they will be standing and remembered longer.

Wealth Made Simple

People are seeking advice on how to create wealth more than ever in history. As a result there are wealth creation companies and seminars popping up in every capital city around the world. Many of the people attending are still looking for a get rich quick solution to their life. They will go there with the hope that they will learn the magic secret and the money will flow. The only challenge with this is that knowing what to do doesn't change a thing. Everybody knows they should save money. Everyone who has attended a wealth creation seminar knows the importance of investing and almost everybody would like to be earning more.

In order to create wealth you must begin with a mindset of wealth. A mind that is conditioned to the accumulation of wealth.

"You create an abundance of wealth by adding value to other people's lives."

Exponential entrepreneur Peter Diamonds says, *"If you want to be a billionaire, help a billion people."* Even if your financial goals are not genuinely so ambitious, you hopefully get the point.

Your wealth, including the joy that comes from it, is in direct proportion to the number of people you help and the amount of value you can add to their lives.

People who like what they do, naturally get good at it. That's why the sage advice of *"do something you love"* - as corny as it may sound, is actually really good advice. But it must add value to other people's lives for a financial return.

Although some people have become wealthy being luke warm about what they do, I cannot think of a bigger waste of your life and your time. At the end of the day you can always get more money, but time is your most valuable commodity. Once spent it is gone forever. Why spend your life doing something that doesn't make you want to leap out of bed and inspire you each day? If you truly value your life then you owe it to yourself to find that passion, that purpose for your existence no matter how long it takes.

I know people who have spent thousands of dollars attending seminars to learn how to become wealthy through property investing and share trading. In my estimation you could interview those people attending one year from the event and find that fully 90% wouldn't have made a single investment. And in most cases you'll find it's because they don't like driving around looking at properties, going through newspapers and phoning agents.

Could you imagine Warren Buffet (the greatest share investor in the world) finding the tasks of analysing companies, its forecasts and future business potential monotonous?

"To be truly successful at anything, you must love what you do."

To get the maximum use of your time and your life you must have that unwavering passion for what you do. Passion carries with it the seeds to belief, energy and enthusiasm about what you do. These are the most influential allies you possess.

When you are dealing with someone who has that passion and excitement for what they do, they invariably gather support. Entire teams are built on these qualities. People invest millions of dollars with people who have these qualities. They are recognised as the qualities in people who refuse to quit. The conviction, determination and drive that naturally come from doing what you passionately believe in is a powerful asset. As you enter the exercises on goals, you may begin to get a glimpse of what it is you were put on this earth to do. I believe we each have a unique contribution to make. Yet it is a purpose that we must uncover from within ourselves. Many people seek the fame and fortune and wind up miserable at the end of their lives because they haven't fulfilled their hearts desire. If you truly want to experience abundance then go for the works. Emotional, physical, spiritual and financial abundance is available to you. You will find it in your passion.

Your list of passion questions to answer -

- What am I most passionate about?
- What are my favourite hobbies, sports, interests and charity work?
- What world issues do I get worked up about?
- If money wasn't an issue, what would I love to do with my time?
- Who are some of the mentors I look up to?
- What is it about these people that I admire the most?
- What qualities do they have that I'd like to emulate?
- What have these people accomplished that makes me respect them so much?
- Are they doing what I really want to do?
- What contribution do I want to make or causes do I want to help? (Commercial or charitable)

Find your passion and your zest for living becomes the fuel that will light up a new world for you and the people around you. People's passion for what they love to do is contagious. The people I respect and am affected by the most are the people who love what they do. They have energy and a belief so strong that nothing could sway them from the life they are living. They are true to themselves. That type of life is the one you too can experience. And you can have it the same day you answer those questions on passion.

"Success is not the result of spontaneous combustion. You must set yourself on fire." - Reggie Leach

Creativity Has Its Place

The entire process of goal setting is almost as perfect as Mother Nature herself. The only reason goals don't work is if we don't work them in the way they were intended to be used. We are the only creatures on this planet that attempt to re-invent wheels and change a winning formula. Every other creature on this planet lacks the creativity that we humans have. Yes, this creativity has taken many to great heights and helped them achieve extraordinary success. If you take the time to look back over history you will find those that have experienced this type of success have all been great exponents of the goal setting process.

Creativity has its place in the goal setting process. It is used to create the vision, explore possibilities and find solutions as you encounter obstacles. When it comes to working the system of goal setting we must be disciplined enough to follow the system of goal setting and resist the temptation to short cut or change a winning formula.

The only reason that goals won't work is if people don't work the system. Sure you can try and slice it and blur the edges rather than do every little single thing that the process of goals asks of you. But who would you be kidding? A polar bear doesn't try to skip hibernation for a year because he wants to do some extra fishing. There is a certain way he has to do things or it will cost him his life. *Universal Laws* must be abided by in order for us to stay alive. It was Cecil B. DeMille that said,

"We don't break the law we only break ourselves against the laws."

If we ignore these truths which have existed for longer than recorded history we will find ourselves with the same fate of that of the polar bear that ignores the signs that the seasons are changing. There are people who have come up to me and said that goals don't work for them. They have become creative where they required discipline.

Work the System

There is a power within us that lies dormant until we set upon a goal and make the commitment to ourselves that we will see it through until we attain it. Setting a goal activates a part of us that we don't even have to fully understand to get it working. We can cure headaches in a split second when we go from sitting around dwelling on it to getting up and doing something different. We can release an abundance of energy a moment after deciding to move. We generate ideas that we never previously thought we were capable of conjuring. We each have tremendous power and the only sad thing I can pull from all of this, is that so few ever make the choice to experience what I have just described.

I am openly ignorant about the finer points of mechanical engines, but I never fail to turn the key in my car in order to get where it is I want to go. The point is we don't have to understand how everything on this planet works in order to use it. You have been using these *Universal Laws* since the day you were born whether you were aware of them or not. Admittedly there are some things we must take the time to understand. I believe the subject of this book and others like it should be taught in every school in the world.

When you set a goal you begin using these *Universal Laws* whether you know them or not. We would be foolish not to take advantage of some things because of our inability to explain how it works. This universe contains a system that works with flawless perfection and all it requires is for you to think and act. You can change your results but not by trying to change the system. We must adapt to the *Universal Laws* and begin using them for the better if we wish to reap better rewards.

"The most flexible person in any environment is the most powerful." - Dr. John Gora PhD

Your ability to adapt to the process of goal setting is just the beginning. The obstacles you encounter along the way will be your second test. All great success comes from your willingness and ability to change and improve.

Pablo Casals, the great cellist, was asked why, at 85 years of age he continued to practice five hours per day, He replied, "*Because I think I'm getting better.*"

Success begins the moment we understand that life is about growing. This is the purpose of setting goals. Goals are designed to entice you to become the type of person it takes to achieve them.

A study conducted on goals that commenced in 1953 at Yale University found that only 3% of the graduates that year actually had written specific goals. In 1973 those 3% were worth more than the other 97% combined. The important thing here is not just they were financially better off, but do you think that they experienced better family relationships, were more healthy and happy than those in the 97%?

If they were giving out McDonald's Restaurants tomorrow for FREE would you want one? If yes, why? Is it because it is a proven success system that you can use as a vehicle to get anything you want in life? If you are like most people, who value financial freedom then you probably answered yes to both of these questions. Goal setting is no different. It is a proven formula. Most would agree with me on the fact that anyone who was to attempt to change this effective system should probably be locked up and have the key thrown away. What's the only reason a McDonald's franchise won't work? The answer-creative people. If you were to try and re-invent the way those golden fries were made I think Ray Kroc would roll over in his grave.

If such a formula exists then why don't more people become financially free, live with better health and experience more fulfilling, stable relationships? It can only be because they do not have the formula or they are not working the system they have been given.

I was reading that according to a survey conducted recently in New Zealand that 17% of the population was obese and a whopping 35% of people were overweight. The number of divorces these days is staggering. We've all heard the statistics with two out of three marriages ending in divorce. I mention these figures not to highlight any particular country but to use it as an example of how we in the western world are living like. There is more than enough information on how to have successful relationships and live in good health. The success systems are there. Ignorance is not bliss. Ignorance hurts. If it doesn't hurt now it will later on. Before we get down to some of the nitty-gritty of goal setting we must first examine the reasons why people don't set goals so that we avoid, as Lester Thurow put it, *"Living lives of quiet desperation"*.

7 Reasons WHY People Don't Set Goals

1. Not Serious
2. Don't or won't take responsibility
3. Don't realise the importance of goals
4. Don't feel worthy of their goals - lack the belief of deserving
5. Don't know how
6. Fear of Confrontation (The biggest fear of them all - it is the reason we fail to face up to other fears and awkward situations with other people)
7. Too comfortable - lazy

Take a minute to recognise within yourself any of the above seven that have caused you to put off your dreams and aspirations in the past. We must nail these things now so that they don't cause us pain in the future. The pain of lost time and regret can be immense.

Write yourself a 'Get Serious Commitment'. I am going to give you a short section of a very personal commitment I made years ago to myself during the very early stages of writing the first edition of this book. After reading it you may get a sense of how I felt at the time. I was working away from my family, struggling with my health and unhappy in my career. After writing this, the letter sat on my fridge and every time I read it I feel the intense feelings in which it was written. It drove me to avoid becoming a victim of the seven reasons mentioned above. It drove me to start a company, step up, get out of my comfort zone and deliver for all the right reasons. And it kept me focused on using this success system.

Here's what it said:

On this day as I sit here looking at the photos of my daughter and thinking about how much I miss her on her 8 month birthday, I make the promise that I will finish the first of my many books so I never have to spend a week away from her out of necessity ever again. The tears that stream down my cheeks, bitter my cheek muscles and pain my heart and will drive me until the day that I can spend every waking moment with her if I choose. A week apart is too unbearable. A day without hearing her sweet soft voice is a shallow day. I vow never to miss the birthday of my immediate family ever again. I sit and stare at the photo of Annabel hugging a huge white teddy bear and I wish it was me. No one has bore witness to the determination I am about to unleash. I mark this day as a turning point in my life. This decision carries the seed that millions of other people will benefit. Below is a list of the things I will do over the coming weeks to ensure the reality I envision is mine. I will draw on every ounce of character I have. I will fight to maintain my health and energy and this glandular fever and Candida can begin counting their last days. Get ready to see what Scott Groves is capable of. This will be the making of my first DREAM! Boldness better get ready to write a new definition for itself. I have to work for myself again. My spiritual and emotional being is finding it hard to persist through the days I have been experiencing with my employment of late. I am grateful to those who are supporting me through thick and thin. The time has come to find out what I can do with the knowledge I have now, working once again on a passion like the coaching days that I cherish so fondly. I will never forget what it felt like to have those kids running up to see me, sharing Christmas cards and gifts with me throughout the years. It's time to be free.

There is not a single thing on this planet that could deter me from pursuing what I love. My family, my freedom, being fit and healthy, and making a real difference in people's lives is everything to me. And even re-working this book over 15 years later, the same reasons make me feel alive. They literally have not changed. That's the power of values combined with goals.

The purpose of sharing this letter with you is to show how one defining moment can change your life in such a positive way if you harness the emotions that drive you. Capture your own highly emotional moments and you will never suffer from the seven reasons why people don't set goals.

WHAT, WHY, HOW FORMULA

What I am about to explain here is critical to understand and internalise. The process of WHAT, WHY and HOW is a process that must never be upset. It holds the answers to many of the challenges you will face as you begin to design and create your dream life. A life that you can experience if you remember the significance of these steps and how to apply them.

'What' Promise

You are going to be asked to set some goals and it is very important that you stick solely to WHAT you want. You must not let your mind deviate to HOW you're going to get it. People who focus on HOW they are going to achieve their goals during the process of writing them down are susceptible to experiencing feelings of doubt and fear. This will naturally restrict their ability to tap the creative genius within. This genius within, is dying to release to you the potential that you house. It is locked up inside of you waiting its release like an innocent man who has been jailed.

Promise yourself that you will stick to WHAT you want. Promise yourself that you will not be lured by the temptation to explore HOW you will achieve your goals.

Why

The WHY is the section that gives you power and drive. Your inner personal motivator if you like. Whenever someone asks me why they can't get focused or make a change that they want to make it will invariably come back to the WHY. It carries immense power. It is totally emotional and for you to influence your subconscious on a massive scale we will be getting the WHY's involved in this section.

How

The HOW's come into play in the section on planning. This is one of the key areas of distinction in *The Power of Subconscious Goal Setting*. Doubt and overwhelm exist in the HOW's.

People never get overwhelmed thinking about WHAT they want to achieve. It is only when their attention shifts to HOW they are going to achieve such great things that minds feels bombarded. The self talk goes something like this, *"I really want to build the house of my dreams but I'm not sure where to start"*. In that split second when the mind's attention shifts to HOW to get started you risk having doubt course through your veins. It is such a small shift in thinking that we barely realise we are doing it.

Let me repeat that when setting goals, keep your mind focused solely on WHAT you want. This requires freedom from thoughts about HOW you are going to get there. We will revisit HOW's in the chapter on planning where overwhelm can do the most damage.

For now the purpose of discussing the *What, Why, How Formula* is to bring to your awareness this process. The design of your life (WHAT) is an ongoing process that will continually develop. As it develops your mind will expand to greater achievements.

Mental Target Practice

As a pro tennis player it was always great to be able to produce an ace under pressure on a big point. The way in which this was produced, serves as a great lesson in success. Let me share with you a simple experiment that you can try for yourself to fully understand this *What,Why, How Formula*.

I want you to go outside and use a lamp post or a tree as a target that you can throw some tennis balls or rocks at. With your dominant hand I want you to pick a specific spot on the tree and throw one towards your target. Now with your non-dominant hand I want you to throw one at the same target.

Without realising it you have just mentally engaged in the same practice that separates the successful from the unsuccessful. You will need to repeat this in order to fully understand this principle and I highly recommend you do so in order to grasp this *What, Why, How Formula*. If you are like most people with any sort of throwing experience then you probably felt more comfortable using your dominant hand. With a new awareness I want you to repeat it and you will notice that your mind has the ability to totally focus on the target (the WHAT) and give little or no thought as to HOW it is going to hit it. With the non-dominant hand your mind shifts its focus to the execution of the throw.

"So what", I hear you say. Think of this in terms of success. Because the self image of your dominant hand sits comfortably with you it has a greater level of certainty and confidence. It can clearly and vividly see the target being hit with the dominant hand and the result is greater accuracy upon execution. People who have developed the absolute certainty have little need to concentrate on the HOW to's. They remain focused like a laser beam on their target. All of their actions seem to flow towards the target without any conscious thought as to HOW to throw the ball. The actions are effortless and work in harmony with the desired result. Our mind simply *"let's"* our body perform the action.

The non-dominant hand doesn't have any less potential to hit the target. Its potential remains the same regardless of experience. The difference is the focus. The uncertainty that wells up from our subconscious shifts our conscious awareness to HOW to throw it, in order to get close to the target. Upon reflection you will find that the dominant thought was not the target (the WHAT) it was the HOW to. When we focus on HOW to's we exercise willpower, trying to force our body to perform a task so that the mind will believe it can be done. This is how many people live their lives. It causes great frustration and anxiety.

Go back to your tree with a handful of tennis balls and continue this experiment so the *What, Why, How Formula* becomes clear. Throw at the target with your non-dominant hand and focus solely on your target (the WHAT). Give no thought to HOW you are going to throw it. Let your mind become engrossed in the object you are aiming for. Then just throw. Regardless of the result, just observe as you repeat it again. Stare at the target and feel yourself moving towards your target and the target towards you. Just let the ball release from your hand and watch the event unfold from a detached viewpoint. Within a couple of throws you will be consistently throwing with an accuracy that you couldn't have achieved in a whole day of throwing if you focused on the mechanics of throwing (the HOW).

Once you can clearly see where you are going with your goals, your actions will automatically work in harmony to help you get there. It requires no force or willpower. Just an unwavering focus.

The greater the clarity in which you see the WHAT, the more comfortable you become with the picture. It becomes a part of you. This is how you develop the type of subconscious image within yourself that allows you to attract the type of circumstances and life you most want to experience.

Goal setting of all types and methods is really about bringing vague ideas into crystal clear pictures that your mind can see as real. Images that are so vivid that your subconscious cannot tell the difference between the real or imagined. It will just do as it is told. Accepting the commands and bringing into reality what is held by your dominant thoughts.

SEE IT SO IT AFFECTS YOUR SUBCONSCIOUS

If you spend any length of time with your tennis ball and your tree you will notice a few things about the way you see your target that dramatically affect the result.

Clarity

The greater the clarity, the easier it is to hit. You can't hit a target that you can't see. If your tree is surrounded by fog and your target is blurred then it is more difficult for your mind to visualise and hold the successful bullseye in its sight.

Once your mind is focused on a single point you will inevitably and naturally find yourself gravitating towards your target as your mind carves away the distractions and gives you a tunnel like focus.

Frequency

What do you think would increase the likelihood of your success with your target, looking at the tree once a day or ten times a day? Obviously ten times a day would reap the greatest reward. It prevents the mind from drifting and being diluted by other daily urgencies that crop up from time to time. You will notice that the opposite of diluted is concentrated.

Increase the frequency in which you see your goal in your mind and give your subconscious the benefit of concentrated bucket loads of thought rather than a drip fed diluted dream.

Duration

If you spend five minutes totally absorbed by your goal you will have a much greater chance of success than if you just glance at it for a second or two.

Intensity

Is your whole being into the target or is it wishy washy. 'Wish-ey' being the operative word. When it comes to the achievement of your goals the last thing you want to do is 'wish'. Intensity of purpose is the fuel. You must want it intensely. You cannot just hope or wish to hit the target you have to want it with passion and vigour. Be excited about the possibility of hitting the target. Intensity has power.

Life like

When we look through our natural eyes we see color and movement. We see things at distance and we can see things right in front of our eyes. Where do you want your goals to be? Off in the distance or right at your feet. As you visualise your goals see them in vivid color, right in front of you, within reach, moving if applicable. Make it as life like as you possibly can.

Your goals are attracted into your life consistent with how you employ these visualisation techniques. The power of visualising your goals with the steps described above will determine the speed of your goal attainment. It influences your subconscious like no other method. Using them sends a higher vibration into the world. You intensify yourself as the living magnet you are. You can talk to yourself all day long but remember that a picture tells a thousand words. Make it real, feel the intensity of the emotions and see it every day as long and often as you can.

No Limits - No Boundaries

101

This simple goal list is a creative way to get the ball rolling. I know people who have been goal setters for years and still received an incredible amount of enjoyment pursuing some of the goals that ended up on their 101 list.

Essentially you need to write down 101 things you would like to do before you die.

- What things did you promise yourself you would do back in primary school or high school that you never got around to?
- What regrets do you have that you could still do something about? (P.S. It's hard to live a life of no regrets - just let it fuel you)
- What exciting things would you like to experience before you depart this planet?

This list will contain a whole variety of things. On mine I have things like skydive, run a 100 mile UltraMarathon and various holiday destinations I would like to travel to. It is a very basic list and many of the things on this list are rewards for the accomplishment of my major goals. You can do what you like. You may have the most important thing in the world to you on your list. There are no rules. Goal setting is meant to remain fluid and flexible. Literally anything and everything can go on this list.

A classic use of this list was best described in a story featured on The Oprah Winfrey Show about a middle aged man who had a list of regrets. He wished he had made the high school basketball team and in his forties made the decision to go back to high school in order to qualify for the team and erase this regret. He talked to the coach and administrators of the school and eventually through his persistence and determination was given permission to try out. He trained with boys more than twenty years his junior. He asked for no exceptions or allowances. If he deserved to be on the team he would appreciate the opportunity. By his own merit he was living out a high school dream. He did the work... and made the team.

I believe we all have goals like this in the back of our mind and the time to bring them to our conscious awareness is now. Life is about living - plain and simple. We should not deny ourselves anything.

Take your time to get started on the 101 things you would like to do before you die. Do not stop until you have at least 20 and add to it each time you think of something new. This is a start for the other exercises we will engage in. Carry your list with you everywhere and add to it any desire you feel. Google Keep is a cool app you can use for this.

You will think of things you really want to do at the strangest times in the strangest places.

You will see things that spark your thinking and capture your fancy that you simply must write down. Never let a good idea slip through your fingers. Too often we think of something we would really like to do and an hour later we haven't a clue as to what it was. It is in these moments that you will cherish your 101 list. It will contain many things that give you the greatest joys in life.

Just looking over the list is exciting because you know that someday the opportunities will present themselves and your 101 list will serve as the reminder to take advantage of those opportunities. Without this list your reticular activating system in your brain may not recognise the opportunities when they present themselves. Take the time to work on your 101 list today.

The Perfect Day

Another fun way to stimulate your thinking, particularly if you have never set goals before is to plan your *Perfect Day*.

Experience the wonder of it. This is your Cinderella story where you can be, do and have anything you want for just one day. There are several reasons why this exercise works so well. The first is fun. It's fun to dream. It's fun to play with your potential and possibilities. Another reason the *Perfect Day* works so well is because it's probably something you've done to some degree in the past. Yet we never acted upon it because of the enormity of what we imagined. For many people the idea of designing their life and achieving a huge list of goals can be overwhelming. The *Perfect Day* is somewhat more believable, whilst extravagant; it's only one day.

Imagine Steven Spielberg asks you to write the script for a movie titled; "*Perfect Day*". You can have anything you want. No limit on money or the people you can hang out with. You can even time travel in case you want to see the world. What would you do?

When I think of the *Perfect Day* I sometimes imagine what it would be like for terminally ill children who get a 24 hour wish granted to them. What would you do if you had 24 hours left?

The inevitable mortality that we all face has the ability to make us sit up and take notice. It should send a strong message of gratitude to help us realise what we have. It should stop us from taking for granted the most precious thing of all... *LIFE*.

Stop and think about what you are capable of doing and what you would like to achieve, then get on and do it. There are enough people on this planet that have been and gone and taken their dreams with them to the grave. They have robbed us of experiencing their genius. They have prevented our lives from improving by never allowing us to share in their vision. If we are at all serious about life we owe it to those who share this planet with us, to give it all we've got.

The *Perfect Day* will trigger this natural goal setting process within the playhouse of your mind. It kick-starts the thinking process where you have zero limitations and you can have your wish for just one day.

Below is a list of questions for you to complete. Take the time to answer them. As you go through this process you will find your mind wandering to other subjects. Just go with it. Let your mind wander. Dream a little dream. Then dream huge ones. This isn't about trying to design the type of day you think you can have. You need to let your mind run free in its own wonderland. Pretend for a moment that Steven Spielberg is right beside you, prompting you to think BIG!

Here are some of the questions you can use to stimulate your thinking -

- Before you get out of bed, what's the very first thing you would like to have happen?
- What's the very first thing you would like to do when you get out of bed?
- If you could have any type of breakfast with foods from anywhere in the world, what would you have?
- Where in the world would you be if this was your *Perfect Day*?
- What type of house, accommodation etc. would you be in?
- Describe in detail what it would look like and what sort of things you would have at your disposal for the day?
- What would you like to do today, if you had no limits on where you could go or who you could be with, what would you do?
- What activities would you engage in?
- What would you do for lunch?
- If you had one million dollars that had to be spent today or the remainder was forfeited, what would you do with it?
- How would you like to spend the evening of your *Perfect Day*?
- What's the last thing you want to do before you go to sleep?

The idea with this is to get as much detail into your *Perfect Day* as you can. You may find that you need to design two *Perfect Days* in order to fit in everything that you would like to do. Great!

The more the better. There are a couple of questions I like to ask people at this point when I'm presenting this information in my seminars.

Did you notice how few limitations or fears you had as you described some of the things you wanted to be, do or have? You were just dreaming. Like a child your mind wandered in its own fairyland where anything was possible. And if I asked you if you would like that *Perfect Day* some time next week, would you take it? If there really were the opportunity available for you next week, would you take it? Of course you would.

Now imagine that you were to design your *Perfect Week*. Think of some of things you could do in a week. Expand on your *Perfect Day* and extend it out to a week. Exciting isn't it? Now if you think that's exciting I want you to think about what it is you could be, do or have for the rest of your life. If I was to give you enough money, the ideal location and everything you needed to enjoy one *Perfect Day* by next week, would you have it planned for me by tomorrow at sunset? The proviso would be that if it weren't planned properly then you would forfeit your future *Perfect Day* and go on with your life as it is now. Would you do it?

Your life is sitting there waiting for you and you alone. You can dream about your *Perfect Day* the rest of your life or you can put pen to paper. Start the process that begins to attract the people and circumstances that you require in order to live that reality. Make a blue print for your life. There isn't a decent builder in the world that would begin building a dream home without a blueprint. We shouldn't expect anything less from ourselves. It is impossible to remember every single detail that even fits into one day, let alone an entire life. You need to take the time to record how it is you want things. Only you have that first image in your mind of what your ideal life consists of. People will help you build it, but not if they don't have a blueprint to work off. Take the time now to fill in the details on your *Perfect Day*.

By completing this one day with the accuracy that only you know within yourself is true, you will move yourself into the top 5%

of people in society. You set yourself apart by developing the reputation to take the time to think about what it is you want. Most people never get that far. You exercise your own discipline by recording how it will look and you do that in a way that someone on the other side of the world could read your blueprint and make a work of art out of it.

You won't think of everything at once. You need to be patient and let your goals grow as you do. Over time you will begin to notice ideas that you initially didn't have the ability to put into words. These are signs of your growth as a human being.

Balance

The Law of Balance says that we are constantly seeking balance.

In order to live a balanced life we need to have a balance of goals. You could imagine a V8 engine in a car that was running on only six cylinders. It wouldn't go the same distance or run anywhere near as smoothly as one that ran on all eight cylinders. It would jerk its way down the highway of life until it eventually burnt out before its time. You may have heard the stories of millionaires who have died unhealthy and lonely. There are many loving families that struggle financially. The truth is that it doesn't have to be this way.

We each make choices that determine how we live. The only legitimate reason that some people live lives in an unbalanced way is the lack of balanced goals. I have sat down with Mothers who have fantastic family lives and they do everything they can to provide their children with the life of their dreams. Simultaneously they neglect themselves in the process. It doesn't take long for them to see how much their family lives would improve if they gave themselves a little more attention.

Because we can't give away what we haven't got, we owe it to ourselves to fill our own cups so we can offer more to those we care about the most. I developed a series of goal categories that I believe help people achieve the balance they often seek. These categories are based around the highest values people generally have. If you wish to create an additional category in order to clarify your goals a little further then go right ahead. You will discover what you need as you begin writing. The eight categories we need to set goals in to live a balanced life are below with some descriptions and questions to help you along.

I recommend a couple of sheets of paper for each category. Sit down for 30 minutes where you can remain relaxed, undisturbed and free to write as fast as you can without stopping on each of the categories until you have at least 3-10 goals on each sheet. Keep the pen moving and as you dig to uncover your potential, the rich vein will come.

If you find yourself getting stuck, just move on to another sheet of paper. Keep writing for a solid 30 minutes. The *Law of Forced Efficiency* says, "*That when you are overloaded with things to do you will begin to use your time more efficiently*". Once again I must reiterate the necessity for leaving off timelines and boundaries.

Do not concern yourself if some categories are more challenging and you can't think of anything in the beginning. In time you will find goals that are important and exciting to you in various areas of your life. Some will naturally be more exciting than others. Some goals will be scarier than others. You will more than likely go through a range of emotions as you begin to delve more deeply into areas of your life you have either neglected or favoured in the past. Ignore the doubts if they arise. If they do arise you will probably notice that you have started to think about HOW you're going to do all these things, when your attention should be on WHAT you want. Keep your mind on the abundance that you wish for. Just keep going and write down what it is that you want. We will get to the WHEN and HOW of each goal soon enough. You will learn how to turn your wish list into a reality soon enough. For now just dream.

TIP - USE ALL 5 SENSES WHEN SETTING GOALS

Visual - How will it look, colours, clarity, etc.
Sound - What will you hear, how loud, etc.
Feel - How will it feel, what emotions will surface?
Smell - What scents and aromas can you smell?
Taste - Can you taste victory? Celebratory Dinner?

8 CATEGORIES OF GOALS

The eight categories of goals with some definitions are as follows.

1. **Family** - things you want to do for your family, things that make them feel good. Material things for family members or close friends. What type of marriage do you want to have? If you're not married, then determine what type of person you do want to be with. What do you want to do for and with your children?

2. **Personal** - things for you and you only. Run a marathon, learn to fly, somewhere you want to holiday. Doing things just for you is not selfish so long as it has balance.

3. **Health and Fitness** - ideal weight, type of diet, fat %'s, exercise program, activities you want to take up.

4. **Personal Development** - what you want to become, things you want to learn, languages, musical instruments, books you want to read, cultures you want to learn about, classes you want to take, etc.

5. **Career** - Promotions, type of work, type of projects, achievements, etc. What environment do you want to work in or create at work? What is your ideal career? What do you want to do? It's important here to make the clear distinction between career and financial. Career is active income. It is income that you have to trade your time for. It comes about as the result of your personal services. How will you use your time?

6. **Financial** - investments, passive income, shares, property. Financial is passive income that is generated from investments such as property, shares or businesses. How will your money make money?

7. **Material** - things you want. These are the toys. There are too many to list here. This list is best used when they are kept for you personally. Some people begin listing material things they would like to get their family here, but I recommend them in the Family category just for focus reasons. Include everything from the biggest cars and houses down to the smallest of material possessions.

8. **Spiritual** - Religious or non-religious, something that lifts your spirit. What charities would you like to start up or contribute to? What causes do you believe in? What contribution to society would you like to make? If you could change something in this world, what would it be? What makes you feel at peace with the universe?

(I recommend at least 1 sheet of paper per category with a gap in between each goal.)

Note:
1. Goals must be stated in the positive.
2. Write them as you want them and NOT as though they already exist like some other goal setting programs suggest. No time lines or dates on goals. Just write down WHAT you want.

Here is a list of questions that may assist you in determining what it is you really want.

1. Are you currently happy with your present results? If no, why not?
2. What sort of results would satisfy you?
3. How would you like to be remembered?
4. If you could decide right now what is to be said on your tombstone, what would it say?
5. You just saved the life of a millionaire's child. He has offered to give you anything in return but not actual money. What do you want?

6. If you had 6 months to live, how would you spend your time? (Who with, where?)
7. What's your idea of the ideal career?
8. What do you want to achieve in your career this year?
9. What would you attempt to do if you knew it was impossible to fail?
10. What is it that you are willing to exchange the days of your life for?
11. What is it that you don't currently have that you would like to have?
12. What is it that you currently have that you don't want?

Purpose

You have probably all heard of the phrase used by children when something happens to someone. They say, "You did that on purpose". The question I often ask people in my seminars is,

"What are you doing on purpose in your life?"

Many people meander their way through life never ever really considering the reason they were put on this earth for long enough to find the answers. I believe we are all here for a reason. I believe we all have a unique contribution to make to this planet and the people on it. What is it that you were placed here for?

Look at the talents and abilities that you have inherited and determine how you can best use those to create lifelong fulfilment for yourself and those around you. The fact that you were given any sort of talent at all means you have the ability to do something special with this adventure you have been given. Every day you have the opportunity to use your unique talents and abilities. The world will never be the same because you arrived here. The questions are, what type of impact do you want to make? What type of legacy do you want to leave behind?

If someone was to write a book about you after you died, would it inspire people to follow in your footsteps? Would they look up to you as someone who was a shining example or will you be used as a 'don't do what he did' example?

Your biggest discovery will be finding the main purpose to your life. For some of us it is to be a great mother or father. For others it may be to invent a lifesaving device or create something that makes every life a little easier. It really doesn't matter what it is, what's important is that you fulfil your unique potential. What is it that would give you the greatest satisfaction in pursuing?

"I would rather fail at what I love, than succeed at what I hate." - George Burns

Find that reason for living for yourself. The passion for life is ignited the day you discover the way you were meant to change this planet. You can set yourself ablaze by finding the one thing that only you know.

"It is one of the most beautiful compensations of this life that no man can sincerely try to help another without helping himself." - Ralph Waldo Emerson

Your purpose in life needs to be something that is going to fill every cell of your body with the feelings of fulfilment and inner peace. Your subconscious exists in every cell of your body. This is why goals cannot be something that you would just like to do. When you strive to fulfil your purpose in life you will satisfy your inner and outer worlds.

Knowing that you have made a difference in this world is an amazing feeling. Take as much time as you need to ponder the purpose of your life by inserting the most appropriate word into the sentence blank below. Use any of the hints below if you need.

My purpose in life is to _____

Achieve	Assist	Build
Care For	Challenge	Create
Direct	Discover	Educate
Empower	Encourage	Enhance
Enrich	Establish	Entertain
Explore	Feed	Form
Free	Guide	Heal
Help	Improve	Influence
Inform	Inspire	Lead
Liberate	Motivate	Organise
Persuade	Prepare	Promote
Refine	Restore	Save
Serve	Stimulate	Strengthen
Support	Train	Unite

This is not a question that can be answered without some soul searching. Why were you put on this earth?

Reasons

"Strong reasons make strong actions."
- William Shakespeare (1564 - 1616)

You can set goals and define your values, but in order to succeed you need reasons so strong that nothing will stop you. Life has a funny way of hanging on to our desires and will only turn them loose to those that refuse to quit. How naive are those who think that a good thorough plan can overcome all. Logically we all know that there will be inevitable obstacles but it is when we are faced with the difficult challenges of life that many throw in the towel as their dream is shifted back into the 'too hard basket'.

The true test is how we respond to the setbacks. The universe holds a tight grip that can only be weakened by the person whose discipline and patience wins out. Eventually the world says, "*We might as well let you have it, you're going to do this or die.*"

The resolve that is displayed through consistent action cannot be denied from the person who has patience and faith, knowing they will arrive. Like a gladiator who is prepared to fight to the death, an opponent's fate is sealed.

We witness the same event in sports. You can watch an event and just tell from the steely look in someone's eyes when they refuse to quit. Even a business person determined to become a success as they believe with their heart and soul that they have a product that will benefit mankind cannot be swayed by the inevitable sidetracks.

The 2001 Wimbledon Final will go down as one of the most memorable matches in the history of the game. Goran Ivanisevic began that week a wildcard entrant with his world ranking low of 125 and a nagging shoulder injury. His form at the lead up tournament Queens was so poor that many questioned whether he should have received a wildcard at all.

Ivanisevic was the dark horse at Wimbledon. His father who has a serious heart condition looked on as he consumed "fistfuls" of pills just to watch his son play. Throughout the tournament Ivanisevic played like a man possessed. Like a steamroller he crushed his opponents to put himself in a position to become the first man in the history of the open era to receive a wildcard and potentially win the tournament. Never in the history of Wimbledon had a wildcard even made it to the semi-finals. He had arguably the toughest draw of anyone, beating names like Carlos Moya, Andy Roddick, Greg Rusedski, Marat Safin and Tim Henman in an epic 5 set semi-final. He now faced the best serve-volleyer in tennis, Australia's own Pat Rafter. Two-time winner of the US Open and a man with a game well suited to the grass. Over the past nine years Ivanisevic had suffered defeat in the final 3 times. You could be excused for wondering if Ivanisevic was ever going to realise his boyhood dream.

Anyone watching the match would have seen the guts and determination of a man who would have probably given his life to win that match. Neither player left an ounce on that court. Goran Ivanisevic and Pat Rafter literally gave everything they had in that epic final.

As the match entered the fifth set, everyone watching knew they were in for something special. Like two heavy weights entering a 15 round battle they wearily fought. The moment of truth came at 8-7 in the fifth when Ivanisevic was serving for the match. He sent down three double faults as he was visibly fighting his demons of yesteryear. The stadium was screaming like a rock concert. Finally Goran Ivanisevic became Wimbledon Champion.

The lesson that we can all draw from what happened next is one that will stay with me for the rest of my life. Ivanisevic eventually prevailed in this historic day to become the first wildcard entrant ever to hold high the most prized trophy in tennis. In his speech after the match he gave away the secret to his success. He said he was dedicating his Wimbledon win to the memory of his close friend Drazen Petrovic, a Croatian basketball player in the NBA who was tragically killed in a car crash.

Ivanisevic had a reason so strong that it lifted him to heights he had never been before. Ivanisevic's reason meant that failure was not an option. In an interview Ivanisevic said, *"People respect me, but second place is not good enough"*. There is something about someone who refuses to quit before he begins.

Goran Ivanisevic proudly wore Drazen Petrovics' basketball jersey as he returned to his homeland in Croatia where he was given a heroes welcome.

Ivanisevic's boyhood dream, his ill father, his late friend and nine year memory of painful Wimbledon losses culminated to provide reasons so powerful that his life will never be the same.

"Nothing can resist a human will that will stake even its existence on the extent of its purpose."
- Benjamin Disraeli

In my seminars I always say that you won't know how much you want something until you *write* down your reasons. Reasons are the steam in the engine of achievement.

In one of my first goal setting seminars with a small group of colleagues and friends I asked someone to volunteer a goal they had to demonstrate the power of reasons. My friend and tennis buddy Johnny Glanville offered. Johnny is Canadian born and his goal was to return home and see his Dad. I proceeded to ask Johnny 'WHY?' he wanted to go back home to visit and his first reason was, *"Because I want to go fishing with him."* I then asked him 'WHY?' he wanted to go fishing with his Dad. Johnny said, *"Because I want to have a beer with him"*. I then asked Johnny 'WHY?' he wanted to have a beer with him and Johnny responded with, *"I want to talk to him."* Each reason led to another as we finally arrived at the point of the exercise with Johnny. I asked Johnny the final question I had for him and as I did everyone in the room sensed what answer was about to come as Johnny swallowed the lump that was developing in his throat. I asked, *"Johnny, why do you want to talk to your Dad?"* He paused for a moment as the room went silent. With a deep breath he said, *"Because I want to tell him that I love him."*

This was a moving moment as one of my closest friends discovered the power of reasons. You can feel the power of the moment come alive as Johnny added the reasons to the detail of his *Perfect Day*. What made this even more special was that it only took a matter of months that saw Johnny go from having no ticket or definite plans to return home. He was able to enjoy his special day with his father and fulfil a major goal.

Once you have determined the WHAT, you add the ingredient of WHY to bring your deep emotional reasons for achievement to the surface.

> *"You won't know how much you want something until you find the reason."*

What Do You Do Now?

In the spaces you have left underneath each goal, write down as many reasons as to 'WHY' you want to achieve each of your goals. Ask yourself,

> *"What will achieving (my goal) mean to me?"*

As with Johnny, you must keep asking yourself the never-ending question 'WHY' until you arrive at the emotional reason. The activities and things that you will enjoy as a result will pale in significance to the emotional reasons you find. Remember we can intellectually 'want' things all day long but it's the emotions that drive our subconscious.

Many people find this part of goal setting difficult as they face up to what could potentially be a regret of the future that is too much to bear. The thought of missing the opportunity of telling someone that you love them may drive you to share your feelings in a way like never before. Reasons bring out the human side in each of your goals. As humans we are all emotional creatures and we are driven by nothing else. Find your reasons and your goal will find you.

A Million Reasons

I have listened to many people who claim their goal of becoming a millionaire only to be stumped when I ask them 'WHY?'

they want to become a millionaire. They don't have the first clue. It's a goal with no real purpose and ultimately nothing to push them. At the end of the day people don't want money. They only want the things that money will give them. The feelings of financial freedom and the comforts that it brings to you and those around you must be definable. The only people I have met who desired pieces of plastic paper just for the sake of it are people looking to satisfy their ego. The bigger the list of things you can come up with to spend, donate and invest your million dollars in, the more likely you are to obtain it.

When it comes to money the *keeping* portion is crucial. If you develop the habit of "keeping" aside money for yourself, you are already winning. Now it's just a matter of increasing that amount each week, month or year. If you are not keeping anything out of what you make, you need to start with that. Few people understand that the amount is meaningless in the beginning, it's the habit you need. With the habit, the amount will increase over time. It's a *Universal Law*.

Next, if you want to do anything with money I would recommend that you find ways to invest it. If you do the numbers on this you will find that at $15 an hour you will need to work and save every cent for just over 34.7 years to become a millionaire. This does not include tax or any spending to survive. This is the dilemma that many people face with a 'labour your way to wealth' mentality.

In reality, many people will make a million dollars. It might take 8-12 years depending on your earnings but either way, a million *WILL* pass through your bank account. Do really well, it may happen every 3-5 years, for some every year. But it's not what you make. It's what you keep and how you use it.

The Law of Compound says that everything compounds. Money invested wisely will compound. Good habits compound. Bad habits also compound. Every reason you discover to achieve your major goals in life also compounds.

If you have a goal to achieve millionaire status then write down how you will use the money when you have it. It's amazing the

number of people who 'wish' for a lot of money but have no clue
what they'd do with it if they had it. You need a better vision than
that. You need to see it or you won't begin the Law of Attraction to
begin moving it into your life. So start with;

> How will you invest it?
> How will you spend it and on what?
> What portion will you donate and to who? Be specific.

Most importantly, how will you show your gratitude for the
ability you were given to create the abundance?

The key to finding the potential that is housed within you is
to find those deep down emotional reasons. Enough reasons and you
can achieve anything. Discover your true ability and give everything
you've got. I am not talking about some super human effort. I mean
if you feel a desire to give something, then give it.

Too many people begin to get hung up on the achievement of
financial freedom and forget about the people who will get them
there. If you are good at making people feel good about themselves
then give that of yourself. If you are good at making people laugh or
making cakes then give that of yourself. No one can ask you to do
any more than that.

**"You cannot give what you don't have and you should not
hold on to what you can give."**

If you wish to become a millionaire then I suggest you
develop a list of a million reasons. Maybe not literally, but enough
reasons that you wouldn't swap a million dollars if it meant you
couldn't satisfy your reasons. The feelings that come from selfless
giving always returns to you. It is a *Universal Law* that is unfailing.
It is those who have the most emotional reasons that are the hardest
to stop. The feelings generated by taking action, giving the best of
yourself and helping someone who needs it. Anonymous charity has
enormous power. The more powerful the driving force the softer the

obstacles feel. Most importantly is the character that you build in the process.

As you list your reasons keep in mind that reasons may include both pleasure and pain but the goal must be stated in positive terms. In other words you can have a goal to become financially free with the reason being because you don't want to spend your life on a pension relying on the government for handouts. Once again list the reasons down to the emotional feeling that living on a pension will bring for you. Maybe it's feelings of dependency or lack of control. Whatever it is you must take the time to list the reasons of pleasure and pain that will drive you to your final destination.

Do not move on to the step of prioritising until you have completed the reasons. You will remember that I said you won't know how much you want something until you know the reasons.

Trying to prioritise your goals without the real reasons would be like trying to bake a cake without the yeast to make it rise. Your deep down reasons will be the catalyst that causes you to rise. You have done so well up until now so follow through. It's the little disciplines that lead to the big successes. It starts with a pen, a piece of paper and you.

Remember there are no prizes for being the first to finish this book, but the rewards for completing it to the best of your ability are life changing. To know and not to do is not to know.

Write down your reasons NOW!

Prioritise Your List

This is the same process as you have used to prioritise your values. Now do the same with your goals. Prioritise your goals on the emotional want of the goal. The logical inner conversation of HOW you will achieve this goal has no place here. Base your goals and the reasons you want to achieve them on the following criteria.

Place the letter A, B or C beside your goals

A - Absolutely must have, just the thought of it excites you.
B - Would be really good to have, but not a must have.
C - Would be nice to have, but not a must have or good to have.

Note: It doesn't matter how many A, B or C goals you have. Use the above criteria to gauge your priorities about what you want.

Some people end up with the majority of their goals on the "A" list whilst others find themselves with only three or four goals on their "A" list. It is simply a list of what you personally want and how much you want it.

Now that you have your list of "A" goals you need to develop an order in which to pursue these goals one by one. Write out all of your "A" Goals on a separate piece of paper and place them in order of importance. For example, 1 - 5 with number 1 being the most important.

People have asked me if they can have two goals as there A1 goal and the answer is "NO". There's a saying in the bible that says, *"A double minded man is unstable in all his ways"*. This means that you cannot focus 100% on two things at the same time. I have personally experienced this diluted concentration myself as I've tried to write and work on things throughout my life. It's like dividing 100% amongst two. You will end up with a 60/40, 50/50, or a 70/30 split. Get the point?

Either way you will never be giving your A1 goal the respect it deserves. If you are serious about becoming a true goal setter you will take them one at a time and get on with it. As soon as you are finished with your A1 goal you will have an A2 goal that will then become your highest priority. As you can appreciate, the importance of patience cannot be underestimated.

A good question to ask yourself when prioritising is,

*"What is the one goal if achieved that would move me closer to the
achievement of all my other goals?"*

Find the goal that excites you the most and simultaneously
gives you the mileage to carry you to all of your other dreams. Many
smaller goals will be stepping stones to the achievement of your
larger goals. Prioritising clears a path to the door of prosperity, health
and spiritual peacefulness. It cuts away the anchor that keeps most
people docked in the harbour of life. Priorities give you the certainty
to know you are headed in the most satisfying direction. You will
never have to look back at what might have been because all that you
are lies before you.

Your Top Ten Milestones

Webster's definition of a milestone is a stone or a pillar set
up to show the distance in miles to or from a specified place.
Milestones act as intermediate goals used to evaluate progress
toward a final destination. For this purpose I want you to think of
them as your goals within your goal. Your Top Ten is best used to
break down your mammoth A1 goal into achievable milestones. The
ability to concentrate on this list will move you faster towards your
major goal than you could possibly imagine. Often the larger goal
means the most to us personally. If we fail to see any progress we
can become discouraged. Reaching a milestone on your Top Ten list
will give you a sense of achievement that will drive you to keep
going. The feeling of getting nearer to the accomplishment of that
which means so much to you - a major goal.

The purpose of your Top Ten is two fold. It will give you the
necessary feelings of intense desire that most of us need to stay
persistent when the destination still seems so far. It allows you to
concentrate on short term milestones that you know contribute to the
achievement of your A1 goal. This will keep you focused. The
second purpose is that it helps you to condition your mind for

success. Milestones like those you will have on your Top Ten list are significant achievements. It gives you the opportunity to experience mini-rewards along the way. The beauty of this is one day you will wake up, tick off your Top Ten list and suddenly realise what you have done. Your major goal will be achieved.

Keeping your major goals in sight will keep you strong. No matter how impressive some people's persistence seems to be we can all become discouraged. It requires vision and clarity of thought to hold the finished picture in your mind. Most people don't possess this clarity of vision when they start out towards a major goal in life. It is something that is developed over time through the past successes we accumulate. The milestones you achieve as you work on your Top Ten list act as the success accumulators you may need.

If you are taking on a major goal in life for the first time then I would recommend the strictest use of the Top Ten. It will give you focus and clarity as you become witness to your own dreams coming alive before your eyes. With each mini-success you will know within yourself that each step is a step toward your dream.

List your Top Ten Milestones NOW!

1.

2.

3.

4.

5.

6.

7.

8.

9.

10.

These will be the 10 goals you re-write on a daily basis. (To be discussed in the chapter on Action)

Note: You have not yet determined any specific timeframes. The process of *Subconscious Goal Setting* is about planting a picture of what you want with such clarity that the subconscious cannot tell the difference between whether it
has actually been achieved yet or not. Putting a future timeframe on it would naturally upset this process. We will talk about timeframes when we cover "Planning".

The Rejection See Saw

Many goal setting programs talk about the importance of keeping your goals to yourself so that people don't drain you emotionally with their doubt. For the most part I disagree with this philosophy. That's right - I disagree. I understand the importance of energy behind your goals. I also believe that if you are too reserved with sharing your goals you may begin to create fears of rejection for yourself. This could prevent you from making crucial contacts in order to protect yourself from someone laughing at your idea. If I had adopted this strategy for my life then I would never have written this book and you wouldn't be reading these words.

We must keep moving forward. There will always be people lining up to tell you that you're crazy and why it can't be done. Sometimes you'll probably think that you're crazy yourself so who cares what other people think. This is your life, your time, your emotional and physical energy so forgive them and move on.

I know of many people who have experienced an enormous amount of confusion with these conflicting messages. I have listened to audio programs that talk about keeping your dreams a secret so people don't disempower you whilst simultaneously telling you about the importance of team building and sharing your vision with employees and staff. It's a bit like walking a fine line between keeping your goals to yourself so as not to give away your POWER, and talking to the people that can help you get where you want to go. The torment and confusion in this area used to drive me nuts. The 'do I?' or 'don't I?' begins to dilute our thinking and overtake what we're trying to achieve. This is why I developed what I like to call the *"Rejection See Saw"*.

The key to maintaining power whilst simultaneously getting yourself out there to those that can help you is best summed up in the *Rejection See Saw* diagram I use on the following page. If you have a high level of self-esteem then you can lower your secrecy levels about what you're trying to achieve. The resistance, rejection and negativity that people will throw back at you will be like water off a ducks back when you have high self-esteem. I once read that, *"The person with the highest self-esteem is the hardest to offend"*. I believe this to be true. I also believe the opposite of this to be true. *"The person with the lowest self-esteem is the easiest to offend."* What I mean by this is that a person with low energy has greater difficulty trying to fight these negative 'Nay Sayers' and are more vulnerable to giving up on their dreams in their moments of weakness. In the past this would have caused concern for someone with low self-esteem and the person who is still developing their vision of their goals.

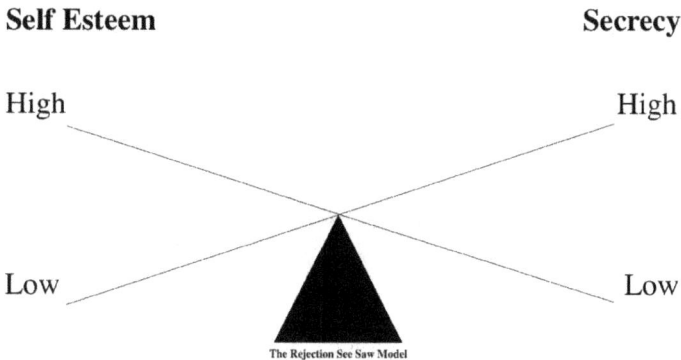

Self Esteem   **Secrecy**

High   High

Low   Low

The Rejection See Saw Model

"It is when our feet are firmly on the ground that we have the platform to push through resistance and reach the stars."

The difficulty most people have in sharing their dreams is that they do it in times of weakness and desperation. When you are in weak states you are extremely susceptible to any negative setbacks. The eyes of rejection and doubt seem to stare us down. This would obviously be the wrong time to be shouting from the rooftops about what you're going to achieve. Wait until you are in a powerful state where you can handle the inevitable "NO's" and knock backs.

Let me share with you a formula for how to release your Top Ten and deal with the rejection and negative energy that you WILL run in to.

"We must release our goals and vision to the world to the degree that we can handle the resistance of rejection."
- Scott Groves

I still remember an experience in high school where an English teacher asked me what I wanted to do when I left school. I told him that I wanted to be a professional tennis player like Ivan Lendl and play on the circuit. He then instantly gave me one of those, *"Yeah right, as if"* looks and proceeded to ask me HOW I intended to achieve this. (You will once again see the emphasis on the *What, Why, How Formula*). I didn't have the first clue about 'how to' make it onto the professional tennis circuit so I answered, *"I don't know"*. I will never forget what this teacher said to me next... *"What are the chances of someone like you making it onto the pro tennis circuit? Why don't you start studying properly so you can at least get a good job?"*

Hearing this was like having a pin driven into my balloon of hope. It hurt. Needless to say I never had the greatest relationship with this teacher from that point on.

I am now convinced that people who doubt us will ask us HOW we plan to achieve our goals intentionally. When we can't answer in the details they would like us to, it justifies their doubt in us. They focus on 'HOW to's' whilst achievers focus on 'WHAT'.

It's critical to understand that their doubt, is a reflection of themselves, and not your ability to achieve your goals.

When you are still in the stages of developing your vision, it is unlikely that you can answer the finer details of 'HOW to'. As a result you should not feel weaker as you tell them *"I'm not sure yet"*. This only confirms to them that we are not capable of achieving it in their minds, not yours. Avoid picking up on their negative energy towards your goals. People who believe in you know that you'll work out 'HOW to'. They'll believe in you and your vision. It is only in our own personal down times when we have been kicked around a little and we have lost some fight that we must wrap our goals in secrecy for a little while. This is so we can build our vision, self-esteem and reserves of resistance again.

The *What, Why, How Formula* protects us from the doubt of other people in one very significant way. Keep your reasons (WHY) for achieving to yourself. Your deep down personal reasons must remain yours and yours alone. Tell whoever you like WHAT you want to achieve. Having someone laugh at WHAT you want to do isn't anywhere near as painful as someone laughing at one of your reasons for doing something.

As your vision begins to develop you become stronger. Your clarity strengthens. Focus has power in it. Your belief begins to intensify and you can then walk through walls again.

This is the stage of your development and growth that makes you invincible. When you are in that powerful state of peak self-esteem you are highly resistant to the negative influences around you. You can walk around like Superman, bullets bouncing off your chest. If someone was to phone you up in the middle of the night just to tell you it couldn't be done, you would come back at them with your own self assuring, *"I cannot help it if you cannot expand your mind to the vision I have"*.

Once you have reached your state of power you will never look back. You have probably already had the experience at some time in your life where you just knew you were going to achieve what you set out to achieve. Deep down inside yourself you discover that place where the glory of the final moment resides. It's like a wave of tranquillity that washes over you giving you the certainty to know you'll arrive. You can feel the intensity of your determination give way to the exhilaration of success. In your mind and body you have already succeeded.

In this state of power is where you will find this. Your *Rejection See Saw* becomes tipped in the direction of your dreams and the higher up you go the more beneath you is other people's doubt.

The point of the *Rejection See Saw* I want to make clear here is that you do not have to wait until you are at the height of your power in order to share your dreams.

> **"*Just release your goals and ask for help to the degree that you can handle it.*"**

Releasing your goals to the world means you are working with the *Universal Law of Detachment* which says, "*To get anything in life you must relinquish your attachment to it*".

Keep working on your vision. Continually clarify WHAT you want to achieve. What it will look like when you're done. Every time you put yourself out there and gather more information, recruiting more help from like minded people, your vision will get clearer. The real key to reaching the power state is gradually working towards it. With each push off the ground you can reach a new height.

Some people have a natural ability to resist negativity and people who tell them it cannot be done. If you are one of these people, great. If you are not, then there is no longer a reason to despair. You have a formula for building your own personal power from within. Bit by bit you can release your dreams to the degree that you can handle it and the momentum and power will grow.

Eventually you will reach a point where your *Rejection See Saw* is pointing true north (straight up and down). In this state you will have mastered your vision and clarity of purpose with this particular goal. You will be invincible to negative feedback and exterior doubts. You will have continued to add to your list of reasons and with it, your own inner strength will have reached a point where you cannot turn back.

When you reach this point of no return with your goals you can tell the whole world the WHAT and the WHY. You will have a purpose. One that is worth dying for and you won't care who tells you it can't be done. You will even begin to hear it less as you develop the inner conviction that shines through and people around you will just know that you are serious and not to bother trying to deter you from disappointment. You will have used the Rejection See Saw to overcome the 'Nay Sayers' of this world and it then becomes just you and your goal.

Release Your Top Ten Milestones

Go public with the things you want most. As we just discussed there are people who talk about keeping your goals confidential in order to safeguard themselves from negative people.

To achieve your goals you need to put yourself out there in the public domain. Overcome your fears of rejection and move forward toward the people who want to support you and help you. The truth is that no one makes it alone. We all need help on the road to success. Many people have perished in the desert as they attempted the journey of their lives all because there was no one there to help them. They stranded themselves because they didn't let someone know before they went or because their pride wouldn't allow them to accept supplies as they launched.

Release your Top Ten Milestones. Tell people what you are trying to achieve. I look at some of the incredible athletes of this world, some disabled, some not, and I notice how their commitment towards their goals changes when someone else's money or reputation is on the line. They put their own personal reputation on the line by sharing their dreams with people who want to see them succeed. Once aligned with people who believe in you, you become stronger than the sum. One plus one now equals three.

Take a chance on those you think will support you. Many will disappoint you. They may not even say it, but you will see it in their eyes. You will feel it through the *Law of Vibration*. Understand that it's okay. It shouldn't make them any less of a friend. Just understand that not everyone has the same vision of what's possible.

It's a quality that takes time to develop. As you begin to share your Top Ten you will enlist the help of people that you never expected come to your aid. Some of these people will be people that you have never even met. Get around these people as often as you can. These people are winners. They like to be around people like you who have dreams and goals and continually think big. They like to be around people who stand for what they believe in. People like you who have that unshakable determination to be all you can be. You will attract the people and circumstances that will invariably take you to where it is you want to go. The bigger the goal, the more fun you'll have with these people along the way.

When you come to the end of your life it will be the people that you shared your experiences with that you will cherish the most. It's the moments of heartaches that you overcome together, the trials and tribulations. And it will be these experiences that you look back upon with the greatest fondness. So welcome the difficulties. Welcome the people who didn't believe in you in the beginning as they begin to come around to your way of thinking. And if they don't come around it's okay. Not everyone wants to overcome the challenges and not everyone wants to enjoy the same levels of success. We all get satisfied at different levels. As successful individuals we come to understand that for some, this level of acceptance is well below what we personally would accept. I guess that's what makes us unique, just like everyone else.

Points to Remember on Goals:

1. Goals must be in writing.

2. Goals must be written without any boundaries or limitations.

3. Let your imagination soar. Forget time lines or what you presently believe. If it already exists, it's possible. If it doesn't already exist then why don't you be the first? Previous experience can only exist in goals already achieved.

4. What, Why and How. The formula only functions in this order.

5. Do not base your goals on your current self image. Think beyond which you are already capable. Think BIG!

6. Keep your goals in harmony with your highest values.

7. Back your goals with powerful emotional reasons.

8. Your goals must be measurable.

9. Prioritise your goals.

10. Make a list of your Top Ten Milestones for the year and release them to the world to the degree that you can handle rejection.

CHAPTER 5

Planning

Vacation Formula

How many of you can admit to planning your lives as well as your vacations? What about planning your marriage as well as your wedding day? How many develop a plan on how to raise happy, healthy, self assured children?

"Most people on this earth will plan for the party but not the existence." - Scott Groves

Great goal achievers are people who hold the long term vision in their minds and work on the daily steps in order to arrive. In this section you are going to learn how to develop a Murphy Proof Plan. This is a plan that will allow you to think with the creativity you need to remain free and reduce the feelings of overwhelm that can arise when Murphy throws his spanner in the works.

Planning is where we get down to details and timelines. Any surprises on that one? If you have come this far I know that you are not shy when it comes to following through. I personally have to challenge myself when it comes to the details of planning. If you are anything like me, then you must come to accept the importance of planning or your grandiose ideas will never come to fruition.

Now that you have completed the section on goals you will understand what I couldn't have put into words for you before. You now know that some things can never be explained in a book. They need to be experienced. People can give you the ideas and point you in the right direction but only you know what it's like when you do it for yourself. Understanding this, you will appreciate what we are going to do here. The section on planning is designed to help you find the HOW to's. We will do this in a way that will keep you inspired by your dream.

People flake it at this point because the detailed work decays the inspiration of the goals. As you would have realised by now there IS something we can do about this. I use an Action Planner that divides each goal into sections.

The key is to keep the continuity. As you work on your plan you need to remain focused on the goal. Put the outcome at the top of the page and write down the three biggest, most powerful reasons you have directly under it. Then go through and complete the questions on planning. Think fast and write at warp speed so the ideas keep flowing. This is critical. You would have found that when writing your goals out, you got on a roll and that is when your inspiration and ideas just seemed to pour out of you. You can do the same in the planning stage.

If you get a bit bogged down in one part simply move on to another question and let it flow. Write continuously for twenty to thirty minutes and then take a break for five minutes. This will help you keep your mind fresh and alive. If you think of one of your most desired goals right now, you will already be able to think of a couple of things that you could do to get you started.

Now I know that we are dealing with a few different personality types here. Some of you will be tempted to continue planning because planning is your strength. Others can't stand planning and will be reluctant to have a serious crack at even thirty minutes.

Stretch yourself regardless of which exercise challenges you. Only good can come from expanding your Circle of Comfort.

The key is to be creative and continue to operate without restriction. As we begin to get into the tasks of what is to be done you may become overwhelmed. Understand that this is natural. The amount of work that is piling up as your plan takes shape with the details of the journey ahead has shifted your attention to HOW to. This signals a good time to stop, re-focus on WHAT you're going to achieve and WHY you're doing this. They remain at the top of your page for this reason. At any stage you begin to feel overwhelmed you simply refer to the top of page one and take a few minutes to get the vision again. It is only in the beginning that overwhelm carries any clout. As time goes by you will begin to get more and more excited. If you have ever built something of significance like a house you will know what I am talking about.

Overwhelm only exists in the "HOW". When your mind focuses on the big picture instead of the tasks, you begin to renew your faith. All great successes are achieved by focusing on WHAT you're going to accomplish. This allows you to enjoy the planning and the completion of each task as you progress through the planning stages. The momentum of each exercise you complete will snowball toward your dreams.

2 TYPES OF TIMELINES

1. Set Timelines

These are timelines that are set by someone else. Although they are necessary for businesses and organisations to function with their relevant benchmarks, as individuals we must evaluate whether the timeline is ours or being pressed upon us. The feeling of conforming to someone else's timeline creates feelings of being dictated to and the sense of being out of control. As goal achieving individuals we look within ourselves to find what it is we want to achieve. Once again we must ignore the inner voice that will be trying to tell you what it believes you can achieve based on what you presently know. The feeling of being out of control when timelines are set by an outside source is best overcome by changing the timeline for you. Why conform to a standard set by an organisation when you are capable of so much more? Shoot for what it is that you are capable of achieving and forget about the limits placed upon you by world records, quotas and the like.

2. Timelines Set by You

The purpose of this chapter on planning is to show you a method where you can bypass doubts and fears. To find out the relevant information you need in order to achieve your goals and to have the plan create its own timeline. This will be a new concept for most to grasp. If you have ever been through other goal setting programs you will get a sense that I am going against the grain here. The old decide upon a goal, set a deadline and go for it naturally creates doubt. It does so because of the uncertainty surrounding the timeline. How can anyone decide upon a timeline without the basic knowledge of the tasks involved in reaching the goal? People who adopt the WHAT, WHEN method of goal setting experience more doubt, more fear and are less likely to follow through as they must constantly conjure the willpower to move forward in the face of uncertainty. Remember the first chapter on the subconscious? Remember the statement that it requires no willpower to achieve your goals? Develop the mental picture of yourself achieving your goal so that doubt remains at bay.

"Stay fixated on WHAT with the fuel of WHY as you map out HOW to determine WHEN."

Subconscious Factor I

You tend to have a different conviction with timelines set by yourself. However, there are a few other factors I would like you to consider before you set the timeline. In *The Power of Subconscious Goal Setting* the timeline will be one of the last things you will set. Why? Deciding upon a timeline too early in the process of goal setting may set you up for failure. What I mean by that is that a timeline immediately triggers your brain to ask you whether or not it can be done in that timeframe. If your brain answers *"NO, I cannot complete this goal within this timeframe"* then you risk jeopardising the remainder of your plan with fear of failure and doubt. Many people will unconsciously experience this at a level below their conscious awareness and continue with their outdated goal setting formula whilst simultaneously doubting the success of their ideal outcome. It is vital to follow the order of WHAT, WHY, HOW and WHEN.

Anything Is Possible

A good way to open your mind to the goals that you will set that are presently beyond what you've achieved is to repeat to yourself the words, "*It's possible*". I have found that developing this simple belief early in the process begins to open the mind to greater possibilities the more it is repeated. Remind yourself that anything's possible as you look at the goals you have set yourself.

As we talked about in the section on the self image, we largely base our goals on what we presently see ourselves capable. Free your thinking. True goal setting is when you can set a goal without doubt entering your mind. Remember that the conscious mind can only hold one thought at a time. When you set a goal to double your income, I want you to repeat to yourself that "*It's possible*". The first step to creating a belief in something is to agree that it is at least possible. You must open your mind to the possibility in order to expand your mind.

How to Plan Your Goal

Take your A1 goal and then list the following. Your answers on this list will become a detailed "To Do List" that will get you where you want to go.

Tasks

1. Information you'll need to achieve your goal.
2. Internal Obstacles - beliefs, blurry vision, time management, procrastination, complaining, knowledge, skills, etc.
3. External Obstacles - negative people, distances, money, etc.
4. Talent or skills you'll need to acquire
5. Equipment you'll need to borrow, buy or rent.
6. People with the expertise you'll need to talk to - mentors, financial, legal, etc.

Timelines

7. Approximate time for each activity. Ask someone if you are not sure. It is good to know how long each task takes to complete.
8. Add the total time for each activity to come up with an overall time.
9. Work out how much time you will spend on your goal each day and how many days per week. I highly recommend six days a week on your goal in order to maintain momentum. It doesn't matter how much time per day you allocate but do something every day.
10. Add 10% (Timeline set by you) to your total time - or subtract 10% (Timeline set by someone else) from total time. This will be explained in the *Murphy Proof Plan*.
11. Set a Deadline / Timeline. Taking into account the number of days you're prepared to commit to your goal and the total time that is required - will give you a timeline which you can achieve your goal by.

Note: If you are not satisfied with the timeline your activities have determined then you need to commit more time to it each day.

MURPHY PROOF PLAN

Set timelines for yourself that require you to always complete your outcome by at least 10% early. We do this to allow for Murphy. I'm sure many of you have heard of Murphy's Laws. There are many of Murphy's Laws and the most popular is that, *"If anything can go wrong, it probably will, and at the worst possible moment"*. It is important to understand and accept this law as an inevitable part of life rather than say that, *"Murphy is just a negative old bugger so stuff him!"* Too often Murphy gets in the way and we must allow for this or get setback with his inevitable arrival.

This is not being negative by the way. It's just that we simply cannot think of everything when planning big goals. If you already knew everything, and had all of the skills and attributes to achieve your goal, then you wouldn't be stretching yourself, would you?

Even if we try to plan for all of the things that could go wrong, we would be spending too much time focusing on things that may not even happen. This type of over-planning is what leads to feelings of overwhelm and fear based procrastination.

"Determine the very worst thing that could happen and make sure that that doesn't happen." - Thomas Watson

Determining the worst thing that can happen is about all the negativity I can take when planning my dreams. I just plan for the extra 10% and if Murphy fails to show up as he sometimes does then I get to finish 10% early. Murphy Proof your plan with the 10% rule.

After writing your plan in detail, all you need to do now is ask yourself if you're prepared to complete those daily tasks starting today until your outcome is achieved. If you can discipline yourself to stick to your plan you will undoubtedly meet with the success you desire. If you cannot commit to those activities over that timeframe you simply need to re-write your plan and determine a new timeline. Make your original plan thorough and do it in good time. Any goal can be achieved given the necessary timeframe to complete the activities required. If the daily activities appear too stressful over the timeframe you have set, simply extend it out a little.

The question of whether or not you can achieve a goal is a question that doesn't even exist with a solid plan. If you are prepared to complete the tasks involved it is only a matter of time.

2 Questions People Often Ask At This Point.

1. What if I do all this and it doesn't work?
   This is the wrong question.

2. What if this does work?
   THIS IS THE RIGHT QUESTION!!!

Just imagine the possibilities of having a formula like this that you could apply to any part of your life.

Using this process may take a little longer than deciding on a goal and pulling a timeline out of thin air but it will give you the certainty to know you will arrive. The belief and faith that is developed with the Murphy Proof Plan will allow you to reach any goal that you can vividly imagine.

Focus

At this point in the goal setting process you have come to the place where you now have laid out in front of you what it is that will carry you to the 'new you'. You can sit back and look at the tasks that you must do and one of two things can happen. You either realise that there is a lot less to achieving what it is you want than you first imagined or you discover that there is a lot more to do than you first anticipated.

This is a crucial stage because it is where your inner conversation begins to kick in and make judgements about your ability to complete your goals. The timeline you now have will cause questions to arise in your mind that will either create doubt or excitement. Sometimes it can be reassuring to know that millionaires actually have a plan to get where they are today. What you focus on from this point forward will determine your effectiveness in reaching your goals.

Here's the choice of focus you will make...

You will either focus on the goal or the sacrifice? If you focus on the goal you will stay driven to achieve. You will tick off each task as it is completed and develop the sense of achievement that only goal achieving can bring. Your self-confidence will grow as your momentum reaches the point of no return. It is a wonderful place to be. Your world that you are personally responsible for creating will begin to take shape.

The danger is when our focus shifts to the sacrifice. This is when we begin looking at how hard it is and what we are giving up in the process. You may miss out on time with your family and friends. You may experience some pains of disappointment, as things don't always go your way.

The pain of discipline can become all consuming as our mind attempts to play tricks on us and tries to make us believe that we are not moving forward when we really are. Our inner conversation begins to try and convince us to be satisfied with what we already have in life and prevent us from achieving more.

These are all signs that your focus is shifting from the goal to the sacrifice and it's one of the most dangerous places in goal achievement. It is a point where many people turn around and return to their *Circle of Comfort*. That place of familiarity that ties you to an existence you previously wanted to improve. One that caused you to make the efforts and commit to the changes and actions you have taken so far. Your inner conversation will attempt to convince you that your life is good enough and the sacrifice to go to another level just isn't worth it.

I have faced this *'discipline of focus'* demon myself as I struggled to come to grips with the difficulties that I encountered. In those moments I drew strength from a very profound quote by Jim Rohn who said, *"We suffer from one of two pains. The pain of discipline or the pain of regret. The difference is discipline weighs ounces while regret weighs tonnes...Suffer the pain of discipline or you'll suffer the pain of regret".*

It causes me to think back over my own life to a time when I had an enormous opportunity as a young soccer player on the verge of possible greatness. I was eleven years old and in my third season at Barwon City Soccer Club. I had been their leading goal scorer for three straight seasons averaging more than a goal a game. It must have been funny watching a bunch of eleven year olds run around on a full sized soccer field. I remember a game where I kicked a goal from half way off a free kick. It was a distance of some 45 metres. Admittedly there was a strong wind behind me. In the very same game I scored from a corner kick as I swung the ball in over the top of the goalkeeper's head (wind assisted once again). I was on cloud nine.

Later in that same year I was selected for an Under 16's Team to represent the region and I was more than four years out of my age group. The end of the story concludes with me walking away from a game that I loved to play because I was scared. The fear of getting hurt by bigger boys. Maybe it was the fear of success? Could I really be this good? Here I was, a young boy with everything in front of me. I had more than enough evidence to convince others that I could step up, but I didn't believe it myself?

> **"How we see ourselves is more important
> than how others see us."**

To this day I look back with the memory of regret at not following through on those dreams. The lesson I learned from soccer was translated into the weapon I have used in my tennis, business and personal life. I have refused to give up on being the best I could be even when the odds were against me. The pain of regret carries with it the seeds to lost time. It is something that both you and I can never get back.

Although I am no longer bitter about my decision to quit, I now use that memory of regret as fuel to persist in the present day. I have promised myself never to give up on that which I have a passion for. I may not be the best in the world but I am determined to be the best I can be.

"Don't measure yourself by what you have achieved, but rather what you can achieve with your ability."

Stay focused on your goals and keep your mind off the sacrifices and hardships. They are short term and get easier with persistence. The reward of a goal achieved will remain with you for a lifetime.

"Determine what you want more than anything else in life, write down the means by which you intend to attain it, and permit nothing to deter you from pursuing it."
- Henry Kaiser

The Pressure Cooker

As you near the achievement of your goals a whole range of new emotions may begin to emerge. Excitement and anticipation will build. In some people they will begin to experience some anxiety as they have come so far that they now have something to lose. This anxiety is what I refer to as the 'pressure cooker'. The closer you get to the achievement of your goal and the impending deadline, the more the pressure seems to build. This is where a lot of people develop fear of failure. It may seem a strange time to experience this feeling but it can happen.

The purpose of sharing the 'pressure cooker' with you is to give you the tools to handle it. The key is what you focus on. There are basically three things you can focus on here - the past, present or future.

When we start out setting goals we become very future oriented. Looking forward with a vision of the type of life we would like to create. As we begin planning we focus on a mixture of future and present. As you get close to the achievement of your goal your mind may be tempted to look back into the past at how much you've accomplished or look forward to the day of satisfactorily completing your goal. I have seen some people get carried away with the fulfilment of the day arriving. They take their eyes off the present actions and skip ahead to the feelings of accomplishment. Now you may be wondering how they can do this when they haven't achieved their goal yet. The reason is because they are so proud of how far they have come already that they are satisfied. They are so satisfied just by the fact that they have come this far on something they never once considered a possibility.

In order to follow through, one must concentrate on the daily tasks more and more as the day of reckoning comes. I have seen people lose momentum in the final metres all because they began trying to feel the satisfaction of the achievement before it was due. It happens when you get this close because what started as a vision is now becoming a reality. As the pressure builds, stay focused on the day to day actions. Develop a compulsion to closure.

KISS-Keep It Simple Scott!

Common sense but is it common practice?

1. Decide exactly what it is you want.
2. Determine exactly what you need to do in order to get it. What sacrifices?
3. Are you prepared to swap the sacrifice for the attainment of the goal?
4. Are you prepared to keep your mind on the goal and off the sacrifice?

People often misinterpret what I am asking for when I ask, *"Are you prepared?"* What I am asking is, are you actually ready now? There is a difference between, are you prepared now and are you willing to prepare yourself.

Many confuse this simple but subtle difference. I know people who will tell me that they are prepared to do what it takes in order to reach their goals. But when it comes down to it they haven't arrived with the preparation that's required. They are saying to me that they are ready to gain the preparation that's needed. If you are prepared to swap the sacrifice for the goal and you are ready to keep your mind focused on what you want then you will maintain your momentum. However if you begin like most people waiting to prepare themselves as you begin your journey you will run into inevitable but sometimes avoidable setbacks.

Think of someone who ventures off on a mountain expedition. If they leave prepared with the right tools and equipment, they are far more likely to be mentally prepared as they would have to envisage possible setbacks in order to stock themselves with the correct gear.

Now let's look at the opposite, someone who says, *"I'll get what I need as trouble comes along"*. You can imagine the sort of journey they will experience. They will become more frustrated, more discouraged and more likely to quit when the going gets tough. They may be lucky to get out alive. If you are seriously prepared you will overcome obstacles with the least resistance. Now I must clarify something. No one on this earth will ever be 100% prepared for everything and you shouldn't strive to be either. I am not contradicting myself here, I am saying what Thomas Jefferson said, "*Plan for the worst and expect the best*". We must do what we can to protect ourselves from the obvious pitfalls and then launch. You must get started or you could waste your entire life trying to plan to the point of absolute safety. The path of absolute safety is the path of the ultimate procrastinator. Understand and accept that every single new venture requires some element of risk.

The purpose of planning is to avoid being 'foolhardy'. Pretty soon though, we all reach a point where our planning slows us down and we must take action in order to maintain our momentum.

3 GOLDEN RULES FOR SUCCESS

1.You must always pay FULL price.

There are no discounts on success. Those who strive for a cheap way to get what they want will never experience the joy that only comes from earning the right to call themselves successful. By cheap I mean the mental shortcuts that we take when we know that we can do better than we are doing and settling for a mediocre result. True success only comes from giving your best. You can arrive however you like at success but deep down you always know within yourself that you have never truly achieved success until you have given your best. Our natural ambition will always tease us to go for more. It stretches us to become all we can be by providing us with hope, ambition and desire. These qualities are merely a reflection of what we are capable of with our inborn abilities.

"The success you seek is on the other side
of giving your all."

Once you commit yourself to excellence and practice the disciplines that success asks of you it will release its reward and success will then truly be yours.

2. Always pay IN ADVANCE.

You cannot have success on any time payment plans. It's a unique set-up where we must become before we receive. As a manager of a sales team I was once approached by a man who asked for a promotion without ever earning the right to deserve such rewards. This person was a genuinely nice person yet hadn't earned the respect of the team or demonstrated sufficient leadership. I believe that when people are ready for a promotion the vacancy appears.

There's the story of the boss who gives a promotion to a young and enthusiastic junior of the company. A man of senior years approached the boss in anger and asked, *"How can you give this young man a promotion when I've got ten years experience with this company?"* The boss replied, *"You do not have ten years experience, you have one years experience that you have repeated ten times."*

We are not in the position to bargain with life and with promises of who you'll become if you can have the success you seek in advance. This is one of the core principles in life that once learned opens our minds to the meaning of what it takes to achieve.

"To receive you must become."

When you really break it down you will see that success is chasing you. As you grow to great heights success will inevitably follow. Abraham Lincoln was aware of this when he said, *"I will study and prepare myself and someday my chance will come."* It is impossible to continue to study, learn and prepare yourself without reaping the rewards. If the company you're working for doesn't offer you a promotion your suppliers or customers soon will, but you must earn the right in advance.

3. ENJOY the rewards of success.

Take some time out to look back at how far you've come. The journey of life is to be enjoyed. You must recognise the efforts you have made and the growth you have experienced. As you journey towards your dreams you'll enter a place that is totally new to you and leave behind a picture of yourself that you only once knew. If you are resistant to change you may experience mixed feelings as you realise that you will never be the same again. The magnitude of goals lies in the person you will become in the pursuit of your dreams. You will be a better person, capable of contributing more to those you love. You will have your own personal success story to share. The price of experience cannot be purchased. You will have become someone so valuable that others will look to you for inspiration. This is one of the responsibilities of being in the Top 5%. It is also one of the greatest rewards of success. What you achieve will never compare to what it is you have become as a person. Your achievement will carry its own sense of fulfilment.

How to Use Rewards to Condition Your Mind for Success

Rewarding your efforts at each important step along the way is crucial to your subconscious conditioning. As part of the planning stage I want to point out some of the most important things you can do to condition yourself to follow through on each of the goals you have set. Success is a habit. You probably know of someone who seems to be good at virtually everything they do. They were good at sports in school. They had good grades and received good jobs when they left school. They have received more promotions than you can even count. As jealous as some people get, you and I both know better. People like this have either consciously or unconsciously learned some rules that others have not. They have developed in a way where they can pick up something for the first time and show extraordinary confidence and competence. You and I can do the very same. The key is to condition yourself for success.

Many of us have goals with a timeframe that is difficult to keep our excitement for over a long period of time. We wouldn't be human if we didn't get a little discouraged from time to time. It's vital to keep working towards the achievement of our goals and not let setbacks and discouraging times turn us away. In the beginning we can fall victim to our own poor habits.

Conditioning ultimately becomes a crucial part of our goal setting because as we develop the success habits we literally become unstoppable. We begin by building one success habit on top of another. By starting with the little ones we then work our way up to the big ones. So how do we take a two-year goal and condition ourselves for success and stay motivated to achieve the long term final result?

First we begin by breaking down the major goal into its smaller parts. From your plan you will find this a fairly easy thing to do. Your Top Ten Milestones will play a big part. Next you want to ask yourself what your level of motivation currently is in terms of time. For some it may be only a week or two. Whatever it is, we need to reinforce our efforts at these intervals. As time goes by you will need less and less reinforcement and the time spans between rewards will broaden.

You will eventually arrive at a point where the behaviour becomes the reward.

If you think of the first time you learned to ride a bike, you may remember Mum or Dad standing on the side of the road cheering you on every time you pedalled a metre or two. A week later they would only get excited if you went half way down the street. A month later they would be looking for one hand on the wheel and so on. Eventually they wouldn't congratulate you at all. They didn't need to. The act of riding was reward in itself. The freedom and self-congratulations were enough.

You may notice that not a lot has changed since we have grown. The smallest achievements are a big deal to us in the beginning. We arrive home from work excited that we did something new or made an important contact. A month later with many successes behind us, it takes a bit more to impress even ourselves.

Conditioning is no different. To successfully condition ourselves we need variety in our rewards. Surprise yourself with an array of rewards in proportion to what you attempt. You don't want to go buy a car just because you made some phone calls. The reward must be the right size.

The next step is to reward ourselves for the behaviour and not the result. What we are trying to do is create habits that eventually are repeated without us having to consciously push ourselves. We want to get ourselves to the point of automatically driving forward in the direction of our dreams without the hesitation and fear that holds most people back. If you wait for the result in the beginning you may find you are still developing the skills necessary so reward the actions when starting out. Your attention will and should naturally shift to the results soon enough.

Finally be sure your rewards are positively supportive. Obviously you don't want to be rewarding yourself with chocolate cake if you are trying to reduce weight. Make the reward support what you are trying to achieve.

Rewards if used correctly will give you something to look forward to. They can be as simple as having a quiet bath, getting a facial or enjoying a favourite beverage. And when the time comes to reward yourself, do it. Take the time to enjoy it. This is an important part of the goal setting process as it builds self-esteem. It helps create an abundance mentality and we eventually become conditioned to succeed. We learn that if we persist there is reward. Our belief builds and many other goals can be achieved in the pursuit of a major goal. The reward can often be our "C" goals. Enjoy this process of conditioning. All we are doing here is bringing some of them to your conscious attention so you can control them. In a matter of six to eight weeks you will be doing things that you would have normally sat around procrastinating about. It's exciting to see the changes in people as they practice conditioning themselves, but to experience it for yourself is something else. Have FUN!

Subconscious Factor II

As you begin to achieve your goals I am going to suggest you complete them in the right way. I know you're probably thinking this is really basic, but as you would know by now, it is the sum total of all the basics that make for a grand life.

When you achieve a goal tick it off. Do not cross it out.

The reason is that your subconscious doesn't like to be crossed out or deleted. It likes to be added to. It likes the feeling of getting better, stronger and more powerful. Deleting them feels like you are subtracting things and you now have less on your list, which our subconscious interprets as less to live for. Add to the bank of your achievements and you will be building on the foundation of each subsequent success. That's why you often hear the saying; start off small and work up to it. It's the same with weights, learning a language and achieving your goals. The key to subconscious conditioning lies in rewarding the little steps along the way.

There is great pleasure to be obtained in ticking off your achievements. You develop a feeling of being in charge as you witness the daily achievements of your ultimate goal. It's a feeling we want to condition ourselves to enjoying. Many people misuse this process of conditioning and as a result suffer with addictions that are negative. You can condition yourself to the feelings of achievement and self-fulfilment. Make plans to reward yourself and success becomes automatic.

Points to Remember on Planning

1. Be clear about the destination and stay flexible about the process.

2. You must work on your goals. It is a continuous process of setting, re-setting and continuously defining.

3. Follow the 11 step plan on How to Plan Your Goal.

4. If you fail to plan, you are planning to fail.

5. Create a *Murphy Proof Plan* where you plan for the worst and expect the best. Allow 10%.

6. Make a list, get to it and begin ticking them off.

7. Plan to reward yourself along the way.

8. Tick off your achievements and add to your bank of successes.

9. Your HOW is never as important as your WHAT.

CHAPTER 6

Beliefs

Many find it difficult to define what a belief really is. If you ask someone walking down the street they will tell you that a belief is something that is true. And in the case of the individual it is always right. Whatever they believe to be true is true, for them. Some years ago I came up with what I found to be a suitable definition for beliefs to help clarify my own thinking so allow me to share it with you.

"Beliefs are really just opinions that are backed by proof or evidence that is either real or not real."

Allow me to explain a little further what this definition means. We all hold an opinion of what we believe is real because we have someone who has told us it is true or because we have superficial personal experience that this is the way the world is. By superficial evidence I mean that we have experienced something once and we then develop the belief that _"This is the way it is"_. Since we never have all of the facts, we are each making assumptions based on evidence that is either real or not real. It was Dr. Billy B. Sharp that said, _"A person will not believe something until they discover it for themselves."_

Many years ago the world was thought to be flat. This belief was so fiercely contested that people died trying to prove it.

Arguments raged until 1519 A.D. when Ferdinand Magellan began a three year voyage and sailed until he circumnavigated his way around what he found to be this globe we all live on.

Now this is such a basic example that its power can be missed. Since most of us have grown up knowing the earth is round it is hard for us to truly imagine how strongly people felt about the world being flat. So I challenge you to go and try to convince anyone over the age of ten that the world is actually flat. You will run into stiff opposition regardless of who you ask. The conviction that most people have about the world being round is just like any other belief that people hold true for them.

History has bore witness to many nations being influenced by the power of beliefs. Beliefs so strong that they have literally shaped the way we as a human race have viewed nations ever since.

I remember reading in Claude Bristol's 1948 book, *"The Magic of Believing"* about a Japanese Naval Officer named Magoshichi Sugino. This man had thousands of statues erected in his honor for being a remarkable hero who made the ultimate sacrifice for his country as a suicide bomber. The young Nipponese were told stories in a song of repetition that lead them to believe there was no more heroic way to die than that of a suicide bomber.

Millions of people developed this belief and during the war thousands upon thousands died as suicide bombers just like the infamous Sugino. However the story doesn't end there.

Sugino who supposedly died at Port Arthur didn't actually die. He was picked up by a Chinese boat and once it was brought to his attention about his much publicised death that was inspiring a nation, he decided to slip away into exile in Manchuria. Even when he was discovered to be alive and well the young Nipponese were still being drilled on how there was no greater heroic act than to die as Sugino had. A deeply ingrained belief, based entirely on fiction caused many young Nipponese to selflessly end their lives during the war.

The War Is On

There is a great war raging on. It is as great as any war that has ever been fought. It has lasted longer and affected more people than any other battle in history. It truly is the Great War. Scores of movies have even been written about this battle.

The Great War that I am referring to is less obvious and more insidious. The dangerousness of this war is that it slowly permeates through people without them even knowing it. Before you even realise it you find yourself caught amongst the battle that is so camouflaged that you didn't even know you were fighting. A battle that rages right above our noses. Mark my words when I tell you that this is a serious battle and a war that must be won for you to enjoy the sweet taste of victory. You may be wondering who you are fighting. I can tell you that it is the biggest enemy on this earth.

There is no stronger, more powerful, potent or persistent enemy than this one. The enemy is yourself and the war that I refer to is the 'war of mind'. The battle of positive and negative. The battle of limitation and freedom. The battle of mediocrity and greatness. There will never be an enemy that you will face like this ever again. And once conquered you will have something worth more than all the gold in the land.

The limiting beliefs that you hold are so well camouflaged that you would trip over them if you were to cross their path. They remain well hidden in the subconscious awaiting release to their destiny. The resting place where they belong. Limiting beliefs are a prison which you barricade yourself in. In order to free yourself you must engage in actions that free men and women of this world engage in. And it is a journey that you must walk alone.

"You may ask for guidance but you must take your own steps."

No one can walk through the door of reflection for you. Overcoming limiting beliefs begins by identifying that which has been holding you back. It begins by looking long and hard at the incongruency that exists between what you have really wanted all these years and what you actually have. The difference between the types of actions you should have been taking to get there and the types of actions you have been taking. Remember that we each operate consistently with what we value and believe.

Many times we try to convince ourselves that we do not suffer from fear of failure. But upon further examination we may find this is not always accurate. Ask yourself the question, *"What would I dare to do if I knew I could not fail?"* If the answer is something that you are not currently pursuing you need to ask yourself the question *"why?"* If there were no fear then surely you would be moving in the direction of your dreams already. This simple question which was asked at the beginning of the goal setting section shows us just how much subconscious fear holds us back. Do you believe failing will cost you your life?

The truth is that our own fears camouflage themselves in shrouds of limiting beliefs. Disguised in a fabric that is the death of dreams. We consciously don't even recognise them when our fate is so obvious to others. This war of mind is asking us to un-wrap the layers of limiting beliefs.

How do you begin to mount the defenses against such opposition? The first step is to identify an inconsistency in behaviours and desires. The truth of our actions cannot be camouflaged by our temptations to rationalise. The second step involves one of several methods. These methods combine to give each warrior an arsenal of weapons in order to overcome the magnetic pull of these limiting beliefs.

During some of the exercises to follow you will be tempted to raise the white flag of distraction and go and do something else. I urge you to persist. For once a limiting belief is replaced by an empowering one, victory is all yours.

Minds are maintained through the habits of thought and changed through the discipline of self-analysis. You must set yourself free by pursuing an uncomfortable battle against denial and cover-ups. There's an old saying that what doesn't kill you makes you stronger. In the long run, challenging yourself to improve never hurt anybody. You will have engaged in a war where the enemy becomes your friend and everyone wins. This is true victory.

Wishing Well

Why don't we desire everything? Why don't we desire the ideal relationship, career, ultimate holiday, large investment portfolio, and desired level of skill at a certain sport?

One reason we might not desire everything is because we don't believe we can have everything. Over time many people have convinced themselves that the so called *'good life'* is for someone else. They have somehow developed the belief that success in life is not for them. Like zombies they walk around with wishes that will never manifest themselves into reality because they lack the belief in themselves that will cause them to venture outside of their *Circle of Comfort* and experience change. It's such a shame too because for most people they don't even realise they are doing this to themselves. To a large degree they believe their life is controlled by external forces such as the weather, the boss, the car breaking down, and the lack of money they have and so on. They have unconsciously imprisoned themselves with limiting beliefs.

Imagine a well so deep and dark that no matter how many coins of hope you drop into it you will never see the pot of gold. Life is like this. Wishing has never set anyone free. Since everyone wishes and hopes for more it becomes obvious that there must be another answer.

Road Blocks

These self-imposed *Road Blocks* that people have set up stop them in their tracks from ever reaching the destination their heart desires. Former bodybuilding champion and movie star Arnold

Schwarzenegger said, *"You must first see it in your mind and then believe it in your heart."* If the head and the heart aren't working together you'll be setting yourself up for a life of struggle and constant challenge rather than creating an unstoppable momentum where you can achieve your ideal life. Remember that emotion is a driving force of the subconscious. This is why emotional mastery is so vital. What you feel affects your subconscious.

Many people refer to the Road Blocks of life as a weight that they feel like a ball and chain around their ankle holding them back or the weight of the world holding them down. I call the Road Blocks that most people face self-imposed, because we have the ability to choose our own thoughts. Yes, I know to a large extent we are programmed at a young age with certain beliefs from our parents and teachers. But to hold that as a reason for not doing better is simply a cop out! It's an excuse made in advance for not trying harder and evaluating what it is we need to do better now.

In an ideal world we would all have been raised by financially independent parents, who loved each other very much. They would have both been emotionally stable, happy, loving, giving parents who allowed us the freedom to take responsibility for our decisions and their consequences. But let's get real.

Very few of us are raised by such parents, and even then, they're not the only people we deal with growing up. So the starting place with all of this is to accept your past and present circumstances without complaint whether you like it or not.

Our happiness lies in making each day better and better, not spending time reminiscing about the past no matter how good or bad it may have been. Yesterday is gone. It cannot be changed and a lot of mental energy can be burnt in the process of re-living some of the things that have happened to us along the way.

If you read on and fail to put pen to paper, the habit of *NOT* taking action will only be reinforced.

"For things to change you must change."

Make the commitment right now to actively read this
chapter. All successful, happy people think on paper. Do not proceed
without doing this exercise. Do not put off your better future any
longer. John Lees said it well when he said, *"Don't become a
knowledgeable derelict who has the information and won't use it to
get out of the gutter"*. Beware of the person who can explain what to
do but never fully understands how it works due to their lack of
experience.

Your time is too valuable to waste. There is no rush to finish
this chapter. Do not set a goal to read this in a certain timeframe.
People who set goals to read a book a week limit themselves because
they never take the time necessary to complete the relevant exercises
presented to them.

Most books offer people the opportunity to make enormous
changes and yet they become so determined to finish the book with
the half hearted promise of, *"I'll do the exercises when I've finished
it"* and wonder why their life hasn't changed. I know because I have
been guilty of the same thing. Over time I learned that the best time
to work on yourself is all the time. There's no time like the present. I
want this book to be a turning point in your life. Take action.

Each time you go back and review the highlights in a book
or re-read a book you will notice that you see ideas in it that you
didn't previously see. This is not to say that your eyes didn't read the
same words but your mind didn't see it. It takes time for a mind to
expand and grow.

Repetition is the mother of learning. It has been echoed for
centuries yet so few enjoy the benefits of this simple practice. This is
why you will remember in my introduction of this book that I said
some ideas will lie sleeping in the pages of this book waiting for
your growth to recognise them. Set yourself a goal to complete each
exercise to the best of your ability and get out of it the changes you
deserve. If you are prepared to do the work then you deserve your

goal. If someone does the work, and pays their dues, do you believe they deserve their success?

The work ethic that is described in the chapter to come on Action is cornerstone to building an unshakable belief. If you take the time to work on the steps laid out in your plan and diligently work on your goal each day then you will develop an unshakable belief in yourself. Each day will build the belief that you can do anything you put your mind to. This is why the exercises in this book are so critical. If you complete the exercises in this book you will find yourself in the top 1% of people in society. Your income will be pursuing you. Everything you want will be trying to catch up to your level of development.

Ask yourself these following questions and begin to shape your beliefs about following through.

- Do you believe that information contained within this book carries with it the seed of power and potential change?
- Do you believe it's worth taking the extra time if it was to change your life for the better?
- Do you believe evaluating your beliefs could remove a limiting step that has been holding you back?
- Do you believe you will get the best results by merely reading this book or doing the exercises to the best of your ability?

If you answered how I expect you would have to the above questions you will now find it hard to rush the exercises contained in this book. If you did you'd be going against what you believe in. See how this works?

Repetition of these questions and answers will engrain this crucial thought pattern deep into your subconscious. It's a good idea to put a copy of important questions alongside your morning mirror. Write them out on a card and go do this now!

The speed at which you move towards your goals is largely determined by the limiting beliefs that block your path. I know people who use affirmations to generate momentum within themselves. They hit an obstacle and then repeat to themselves "*I can do it, I can do it*". They repeat it over and over until they generate enough speed to run head first into their own *Road Block* once again a little further up the road. Each time they nudge this metaphorical *Road Block* a little closer in the direction of their dream they simultaneously experience the pain and frustration of their own obstacle. I am not suggesting that affirmations don't work. Quite the contrary. *The Power of Subconscious Goal Setting* is about an orderly process designed to eliminate these doubts and frustrations. Affirmations are powerful and can help in many areas with regards to your goals. But wouldn't it make more sense to simply remove the *Road Block* allowing you to drive down a clear path rather than head butting your way through a brick wall bit by bit?

The correct use of affirmations is discussed at length in the chapter on self-talk as their importance in programming the subconscious cannot be overlooked.

Turning Point

When people experience what is commonly referred to as a turning point in their lives, what they're actually experiencing is a change of belief. This change of belief can be produced either internally or externally. An example of an external belief change would be someone who is hoping for a promotion at work. As much as they would like a promotion they don't actually believe they are worthy or perhaps capable. Some people have had the experience of suddenly believing they were capable of holding a certain position after witnessing a co-worker (who they see on the same level as themselves) being promoted to the position they had been longing for. The belief, "*If he can do it, I can*" finally kicks in. After externally witnessing someone take the position that they previously believed was out of their reach, they now believe they are capable of the same work their peer is now doing.

A personal example of an external belief change would be a time when I went into a tennis match at a large tournament. I had made it to the quarter finals and was due to play a guy named Mark who was ranked higher than me and who I always considered a better player. He had beaten players that I didn't see myself beating. In short, I believed he was better than I was.

During the early stages of the match the games were even. Mark was serving and I decided to let loose on a few returns. It turned out that the chances I took paid off. I ripped a couple of scorching winners and broke his serve. In the next game I was serving for the set and I won the first set. This was just the beginning.

The second set was similar to the first. Games went by and we were once again neck and neck. When we got to 4-4 I decided to take a chance on Mark's serve again. Once again it paid dividends and I broke serve. Except this time I had to come out and serve for the match.

At this point, believe it or not, I still did not believe with absolute conviction that I could win this match. I knew there was a chance but I still had to win my serve. Fear, doubt and uncertainty (lack of belief) were pulsing through my veins. Mark missed a couple of returns and it happened. I had beaten a guy I deep down didn't expect to beat. The truth was that he gave me the victory through his mistakes. I didn't exactly play great tennis to beat him. Throughout the entire match my self image as a tennis player was pulling me back into a defeat mentality.

The external result was that I could beat him. The proof was now on paper. Everyone could see it. Most importantly, I could see it with my own eyes. I walked away from that now knowing that I could beat this guy.

A few months later I was drawn to play Mark again. Can you predict the difference? I walked onto that court knowing with absolute certainty that I could beat him. I had already done it once but I never would have believed it unless he made the mistakes to hand me the first victory. The external result had controlled the way I was thinking. By the way, I did beat him again. And this time it was without the uncertainty.

The important lesson to take out of this is how the turning point was created. It is basically induced or instigated by a force other than your own self-evaluation. A glimpse of possibility may have existed in my mind during that first match but that is a far cry from a deep down belief.

The challenge with living this way is we may be waiting a very long time before circumstance decides to favour us. For me it was like standing on the side of the road hoping things would go my way before the belief was created. External belief changes can take forever or never come at all. If you remember the chapter on the mind you will realise that this is when results or outside circumstances are in control of our thinking. We are being dictated to by an outside force, rather than creating the thoughts to support the feelings we would like and thus, the result.

These are both simple examples of external belief changes. Looking back over your own life you may realise that you have had opportunities like this already and still failed to take the bait.

External circumstances may favour us and we consciously reject them because we still don't see ourselves as worthy. These beliefs are strong subconscious beliefs and we must learn to create beliefs to support the results we would like. That's right, beliefs can be created.

Internal Change

On the flip side to external belief changes are internally changed beliefs. This happens when someone evaluates his or her current beliefs. Internal belief changes occur when you realise something within you that has been holding you back. It may be out of sheer frustration or blissful relaxation. Those who have experienced this, liken it to being hit by a lightning bolt. It's like a whole new world has opened up to them, which is exactly what has happened. One of America's leading authority of human potential Brian Tracy explains the *Law of Belief* as, "*Whatever you believe with feeling becomes your reality*".

This lightning bolt has in essence changed someone's reality. They suddenly believe they can do it. They suddenly see the path of their journey clear and free of self-imposed *Road Blocks*. For a lot of people though, their turning point hits them by chance. An external opportunity clears the path for them. However we can all do this for ourselves.

Whether there is a road to every destination or we are given the task of creating it ourselves, there will always be a way to get where it is you want to go. Are you bold enough to go where you have not gone before?

Removing your own self-imposed Road Blocks frees you up to chase your dreams uninhibited by your own limitations. You can now travel towards your desired destination with greater clarity, confidence and speed. Free yourself from your own ball and chain and walk the journey of life like a person that is for the first time, free.

How to Identify a Belief

Beliefs are not difficult to identify. If anything it's determining how those beliefs are affecting us that really matters. Let's begin with identifying what are generally referred to as global beliefs. These are beliefs that are common sayings or generalised statements that are often heard on many parts of the globe. They are generally sentences that begin with-

- Life is ...
- People are ...
- I am ...

Also a myriad of common sayings, analogies and metaphors such as ...

- Money doesn't grow on trees
- Save your money for a rainy day
- Don't rock the boat
- A leopard can't change it's spots
- If you climb too high you will fall
- Better to be safe than sorry

Beliefs such as *'life wasn't meant to be easy'* are beliefs reserved for people who have chosen to forever face struggle and never get ahead without difficulty and challenge. I have the privilege of knowing some very successful people and they tend to believe that *'life is an adventure'*. In fact I know of very few successful people who believe otherwise. Something that on the surface appears to be such a subtle difference can actually become the controlling force in our lives.

All of our behaviours, actions and decisions are based upon what we value and believe.

People who believe they are *'too old'* to do certain things in life will invariably make decisions based around what they believe. Although there may be some physical limitations as we age (most of these are also overestimated), anyone who is willing to change the way they think is capable of creating their own reality. Many of the childhood dreams we continue to envision from time to time are still within our grasp. If we can learn to let go of the doubts and become believers again, then anything becomes possible.

Contradictory Beliefs

There are also common sayings that people have mentally 'doubled up' on in areas of their lives that create contradictory beliefs. Two generalisations with opposing meanings can create mental confusion. For example someone may simultaneously believe that you should;

> 'Look before you leap'
> Whilst
> 'He who hesitates is lost'.

Can you imagine the sort of decision-makers they would be? They may also believe that;

> 'First impressions last'
> And
> 'You can't judge a book by its cover'.

You probably have a circle of friends that will let you know when you are contradicting yourself. If you hear any hints of such an accusation then use it as an opportunity to evaluate what you believe. If your circle of friends are too polite to say anything then let them know about your journey of self discovery and encourage them to speak up. It is through this questioning that you will put yourself in the position to choose the most empowering alternative.

Ground Rules

Ground rules present themselves a little differently from the global beliefs we have discussed. They are very easy to identify because they always present themselves with the same type of language. That's right, they have a language all of their own. You can identify ground rules by the words, *"if, then" or "In order to...I must have..."*

For example, *"**If** you loved me **then** you would take the garbage out without me having to ask you." "**If** I could meet the right* *people **then** I would be successful." "**If** I had money **then** I could make money." "**If** you climb too high **then** you might fall."* These ground rules exist in many family homes. *"If you're not home by eight o'clock then you will be grounded."* Maybe it's these ground rules that coined the term 'grounded'.

Ground rules are basically the broad category under which many rules for the different areas of life we have are made. Let's explore these now.

Personal Rules

Each of us has a series of rules that we use to determine our level of success in the areas of our lives. This is how the definitions of success can vary so greatly from one person to another. A mother might say that success is raising healthy happy children. A single male who works on Wall Street may define success as a certain income level that is to be attained before he feels successful. Each of us has criteria that we subconsciously use in order to evaluate things such as happiness, love, family life, career, success and so on.

Personal Rules are no different from ground rules. They are easily distinguished by the words, *"If... Then"* as we have already discussed. It is enlightening to observe the language you use with regards to the categories I have just mentioned above.

When you talk with your spouse take notice of any *'love rules'* that you may be putting in place to gauge the success of your relationship. *"**If** you loved me **then** you would do the dishes without me asking"*. "If you loved me, you'd do X for me" can be poisonous statements that slowly leak into relationships and damage feelings over time.

These statements may have nothing to do with how you really feel about your partner. Yet if you don't catch these *'love rules'* in the act, you could continue to play out this blame game. Eventually you would believe that your love for one another is diminishing over something so trivial. Trivial since you recognised it, potentially disastrous had you not.

"*If, then*" beliefs are the opposite of unconditional love.

How many people do you know who do this?

Our personal rules can create a dangerous game where no one comes out a winner. Pay attention to the types of "*If... then*" statements that you are making with the people you care about the most.

Replace your relationship "If ... then"

With

"When you ... I feel"

We could each improve the way we speak to one another and one of the best ways of doing it is by replacing our "*If... then*" with a "*When you...I feel*" statement.

Instead of saying, "*If you really loved me then you would take out the garbage*", try exercising a little compassion and understanding and treat those who are important to you in a way that they want to do the right thing. The words, "*When you forget the rubbish I feel as though I'm being taken for granted*".

The key expression is the words "*I feel*" because it's difficult to argue with the way someone is feeling. If you use the word '*think*' instead of '*feel*' you are more likely to create an argument. In other words if you were to say, "*When you forget to take out the rubbish I think you are taking me for granted*". This is quite confronting and people are much more likely to challenge your thinking.

You are probably wondering why I have included this in a book on achieving goals. The reason is simple. The people you surround yourself with have a large impact on your energy. Having a supportive open relationship where there is understanding and respect is a great foundation to the achievement of many wonderful things in life. You will find that when you arrive at the end of your life it will be the people that you have shared these experiences with that you cherish the most. Toys and money will come and go, people will leave footprints in your heart.

Success and Happiness Rules

Do you believe you have a greater chance of being successful if you already see yourself as successful, or still waiting for external results to indicate that you are successful? The person who sees themselves as successful already has the greater confidence and belief and will act consistently with how they see themselves.

Like the other rules already discussed we each have a set of rules that determine how successful we each feel. I have uncovered many of these beliefs with people in my seminars and you would be amazed at what some people would have to do in order to feel successful.

For example...

If I had a six figure income
If I had a close knit family
If I had a better marriage
If I had my house and car paid out
If I could travel twice a year
If my health was better
...then I'd feel successful.

These rules, whilst achievable are difficult to satisfy. What I mean by that is that if you were to take their travel and health out of the equation then this person would begin to feel less successful. Or they may have every area satisfied and then suddenly lose their six figure income, ultimately affecting how successful they feel.

I personally have developed rules for myself in the most important areas of my life so that they are easy to satisfy. Why? Because I want to feel successful all of the time. I know that when I feel successful I act with more confidence and boldness. I am in a far better position to negotiate and confront the types of rejection that someone like me faces. I enjoy putting myself into situations where I can create new business and interest people in new ideas. The consequences are the rejection I face as I come across people who may not share the same vision.

The rule I have for success is simple. Rather than have a whole list of things to satisfy I have narrowed my list down to one. And I have done it by taking a good hard look at some of the things that used to be on my list. I used to believe that my income was a reflection of how successful I was. Once I stood back and really thought about it I found it misleading. I literally used this process on each of the rules that I had for success until I didn't have any rules left at all. Then I came up with the one rule that would be easy to satisfy on a daily basis. Here it is...

If I am learning every day and applying what I know, then I am successful.

I encourage people to do this with areas such as success and happiness. Some people carry rules for happiness that are even more difficult to satisfy than their rules for success. Write them all down and demolish them one by one until you have the simplest rule that can be satisfied on a daily basis. If you want to go through life happy and successful all the time, you can. Every day above ground is good enough for me to be happy. I still catch myself from time to time when things don't go my way. However, the importance of this lesson is developing the ability to recognise this "If ...then" process when it begins. This way you can pull yourself up if necessary.

The way you feel influences your subconscious mind more than any other method we have covered. We must remember that emotions are the driving force behind our subconscious conditioning and to what you give the emotion to, you give the power.

Dispute on Paper

The next exercise is a short one that can be used at varying times. I call it "Dispute on Paper". I will use financial beliefs for the examples to follow as I believe it is the greatest area of misunderstanding in most people's lives. Let's take the saying of *'Save for a rainy day'*. Many people have heard this popular saying as they were growing up. However the deep subconscious interpretation of this statement has a more sinister effect than we first realise. Let's take a look.

What do most people associate to a rainy day? Doom and gloom. If you associated doom and gloom to a rainy day then what would you subconsciously be saving for? You would be saving for doom and gloom. Your money would be sitting there in case something goes wrong. Over time through repetition, people can literally begin to associate doom and gloom to saving money.

"The meaning that you associate to something determines how you feel about it."

This commonly used global belief develops a mentality that limits our thinking and restricts our vision. Just think of how differently someone would behave if they were saving for opportunity. Can you imagine the different set of glasses these two people would have on? On the surface it appears so harmless but what you associate to things has a powerful influence over you. To dispute this on paper I would ask you to write down what you associate to opportunity so you could enjoy saving money. For many people I find they turn it into, *"Save for a sunny day"*. This works for me!

How to Change a Belief

In my experience there are two very common limiting beliefs that hold most people back. Obviously there are many significant others that exist within individuals which I'll help you to identify as we progress. But let's start with the two main ones. You get these cured and you're well on your way to your better future where you can have whatever your heart desires.

First, let's start with your A1 goal. Now ask yourself this question;

Do I believe I'll have or achieve... (my A1 goal)...by...?

Take your time to think through your answers. Be totally honest with yourself. The temptation to cocoon ourselves in comfort rather than face our own personal shortcomings takes courage.

The second question I want you to ask yourself is;

Do I believe I deserve... (my A1 goal)...by...?

Once again honesty is the key. Do not skip what appears on the surface to be such a simple question. I'll never forget hearing Jim Rohn say, *"Success is doing what the failures won't do"*. Ask yourself, would a failure take the time to do these exercises? The answer is obvious. Take the time right now to really evaluate your beliefs about your present A1 goal.

The most difficult thing I found with this process was overcoming my own denial. Many people are susceptible to doubt when they first begin. We all think we are positive, which may be true, but the fact remains that probably everybody has some form of limiting belief in some area of their life. It's quite all right if you don't fully believe when you first start out. Whilst belief can develop over time, I would like to show you a way to change a belief more quickly. Let's get serious, let's get honest and let's grow.

To change a limiting belief you need to accept a different reality as we'll talk about in a minute. It's easy to sit there and argue with me on a number of the things you will do here. For example, *"This isn't going to work"*.

If you believe that then CONGRATULATIONS, you've just identified a limiting belief. The reason it's so easy to argue is because people tend to be very passionate about their beliefs. It's the cause of many wars that we witness worldwide on an ongoing basis. Our inability to accept a different point of view is likely to be the cause of many of your own personal wars. Why do you think the opposite of this is called 'Peace of mind'?

Now let's accept a different reality for just a minute. Accept that maybe this could work. The ideal way to approach these exercises is, *"Maybe this could work for me, so I'll give it a go"*. How would I act if I did believe I could attain this goal by the date specified? How would I feel knowing and believing with all my heart that I do deserve my goal?

"The day you believe you can, you will." - Scott Groves

Permit me to elaborate. When someone believes something won't work they shut down the mind to any other possibilities, thus stifling their creativity and definitely limiting their future. When someone accepts a statement such as *"This seems too good to be true"*, many will fail to seize the opportunity because they imagine the outcome having a false victory that can only end in disaster. It represents a deep down emotional feeling of unworthiness as though,

"Nothing this good should happen to someone like me". This makes the exercise of moving forward not worth the effort to do it in the first place because they believe they will only end up disappointed in the long run. This mindset dooms people to lives of mediocrity when they wish with every inch of their body for the good life with all of its wonders of prosperity, health and happiness. Their belief becomes their own personal prison.

Other people may realise the benefit in an opportunity, but because it seems so simple they allow themselves to put it off. They believe that opportunities this good are reserved for people more worthy. What they don't realise is that opportunities present themselves many times a day. They are almost always presented to each of us in the most simplistic fashion. All successful people know that it's the taking of all the smaller opportunities that open the door to the larger ones. The belief is that, *"Any step is better than no step. So long as I keep moving forward, I will find the opportunities I am looking for"*. This is characteristic of all high achievers. They don't stop to let over-caution paralyse them like those who are continually missing out on the gifts life presents them. Opportunities are there for the taking.

> **"Good things come to those who wait, but it's only the stuff left over from those who dared to seize."**
> **- Abraham Lincoln**

A limiting belief can prevent you from even noticing your true potential in the first place. Limiting beliefs are like blinkers that prevent you from seeing your own true greatness. Your future is too important to put off this crucial self-analysis any longer. I want you to use the power of autosuggestion and repeat to yourself every day, *"I can have my goal and I do deserve it"*. Enjoy your journey. I truly believe you deserve the best life has to offer. I want you to BELIEVE that!!!

What Are You Making?

There are light years between making a living and making a difference. This is where the power of purpose cements itself. If you are following your hearts desire and working on some purpose that you believe in, you literally transform yourself. Your belief in yourself is almost put on hold because you have something to contribute to the greater good. It's as if your life's purpose cares little about what you believe. Your inner core seeks a path of higher fulfilment and whether you believe you can get there or not becomes irrelevant. You have finally found something worth failing for, worth sacrificing for and as long as you believe in your purpose as being good and noble to yourself and mankind then nothing will stop you.

For me personally I have found no greater pleasure than contributing to others. I am passionate about helping people make their dreams come true. I know that until the day I die I will study and share the power of the subconscious so others can achieve amazing things. My heart and soul goes out to people and that's all that matters. It's not about the money or being on stage. For me it's about making a difference. I can use my time in no better way than by helping people discover their unique potential and how to maximise it.

You will find your purpose in life filled when your daily activities are invested in something you believe in. A purpose that makes a difference to others.

Identify Limiting Beliefs

Make a habit of identifying any limiting beliefs that you may have. You will recognise words such as "CAN'T" or "IMPOSSIBLE" that may surface in your vocabulary from time to time. If you find yourself saying that something can't be done then stop and analyse why it is you believe it can't be done. Stop yourself and think about the false evidence that you have been using to support this perception of reality. Be open minded enough to tap your creativity and willing enough to pursue other realities. Identifying a limiting belief is the starting point of change. I have a saying I share with people that says,

> *"If it has already been done then you can do it; and if it hasn't been done then why don't you be the first."*

Willpower and Why It Doesn't Work

Whenever someone has to exert willpower in order to try and reach their goals they are in effect fighting their own self image. The image you have of yourself is a picture that you have developed over a period of time. It is your perception of yourself, and perceptions can be deceiving. Because you believe this picture of yourself is accurate, your subconscious will base its actions on this picture. You can only call on the talents and abilities you believe you possess when handling the twists and turns of life. But ask yourself, *'Is who I see myself as, really an accurate image of me?'*

When you recruit willpower, you are actually saying that you need something beyond what you currently have in order to outperform what you usually achieve. Think about this for a minute. Would you call upon your willpower if what you were setting out to achieve was well within what you saw yourself capable? Let's take losing weight as an example. Would you require willpower if you believed you were a healthy eater? Would you require willpower if you believed exercise was exhilarating, fun and part of any normal persons' daily routine?

If you believe that it takes eternal vigilance, unwavering discipline, an impeccable diet and a supportive partner to maintain a healthy weight, then almost everyone would struggle with weight. We can create the associations and beliefs we need to make anything as easy as we want it to be.

Cathi a close friend of mine approached me because she wanted to stop smoking. In just one session we were able to free her from her addiction by removing an erroneous belief. This is the same principle which applies to any addiction. The mental addiction is almost always harder to overcome than the physical aspects. I began by asking Cathi a question I want you to ask yourself. *"Do you believe it takes willpower in order to stop smoking?"* Once I explained to her that it doesn't require willpower any more than it requires concrete to bake a cake she was able to open her mind to change.

I went on to explain that it was how she sees herself that makes the difference. To begin to see herself as a non-smoker who feels zero attraction to those "death sticks". Any non-smoker knows they can see someone smoking without any temptation to have one.

Success is any area of your life is no different. Do you believe it takes willpower to be successful? Or is it the natural actions one would engage in if they already saw themselves as successful?

Whilst a smaller self image with willpower may be strong, it must have undivided attention on the task at hand. Any loss of concentration will cause you to slip back down like a piece on a snakes and ladders game. You call on all of your will to begin climbing the ladder of success until your limiting beliefs bite you on the ankles once again.

You can climb all day long if you like but the beliefs that are held in the subconscious are always stronger than willpower because the self image is operating 24/7 and is ruthless in its execution. Willpower has lapses. It is a weak substitute for the type of programming that you need to reach your goals.

The subconscious conditioning of old which is made up of the beliefs we have accumulated along the way must be re-engineered so that you permanently expand the picture you have of yourself. When your beliefs change, the perception you have of yourself changes. You see yourself and the world differently. Once you have learned how to expand the picture you have of yourself you can begin to climb to a height greater than you have ever felt comfortable with before.

When you learn to do this, you will have learned to activate your automatic success mechanism in every situation that presents itself.

If you have ever been in that state of 'flow' that athletes refer to as "in the zone" you will know how effortless it is. You are no longer fighting old conditioning.

You have lifted the lid on what you thought you could achieve. The sphere of control is expanded in direct proportion to the mental image one has.

As you develop this ability with the ideas presented in this book you'll find yourself moving past obstacles that formerly restrained you. Goals that once seemed far-fetched will suddenly look achievable. Your mind becomes a magnet to possibilities. Once the padlocks to the door of the subconscious are removed you are free to run uninhibited.

"The difference between whether you make it or not, has only to do with whether you believe you can or not."
- Scott Groves

Points to Remember on Beliefs

1. Beliefs are opinions you hold as true for you.

2. Create your own turning points in life.

3. Internally change your beliefs or you may wait forever.

4. Watch the rules "If ... then".

5. Set the ground rules for your success and happiness.

6. Believe you can achieve - believe you deserve.

7. Seize opportunities with the belief you are closer to success.

8. Do more than make a living - practice making a difference.

9. Forget the "If he can do it, so can I" - Believe and be first.

10. Doubt your doubts. Doubt is the opposite of belief. Doubt is also just an opinion.

11. Forget about willpower and build the belief system that will create the fact. See yourself already there.

> *"A person will not believe something until they discover it for themselves." - Dr. Billy B. Sharp*

CHAPTER 7

Action

"In every work of genius we recognise our own rejected thoughts."
- Ralph Waldo Emerson

What does eating, sleeping and breathing have in common? The answer is that they are all absolutely crucial for our survival. They are all things we must do on a daily basis in order to remain in a state of wellness. If for just one day you try to cease any one of these activities your body instantly begins to suffer. Particularly if it's breathing that you attempt to shut down for a day. The *Law of Reversibility* states that, *"Actions generate feelings and feelings generate actions"*.

This means that we mentally begin to suffer as our physical body ails. Our physical body will begin to suffer if we mentally neglect ourselves. A weak body therefore lacks the ability to concentrate with a high intensity. This in turn affects your financial and emotional well being. You cannot lack in one area of your life and expect every other area of your life to be healthy. The *Law of Life* says, *"That if you're not growing, you're dying"*. These are *Universal Laws*.

Nothing in nature stands still. Your life is no different from your body. If you are not growing in strength then you are degenerating.

And so it is with our goals. To be successful and live our lives in the way it was intended we must work on our goals each and every day.

> *"If you are not pursuing your goals you are literally committing spiritual suicide." - Les Brown*

Your inner being has a sense of whether or not you are chasing your hearts desire. Deep down each of us knows that what we are doing in this present moment has the potential to move us in the direction of the life we want. Either that or it's moving us in the direction of a life we don't want. Sometimes it's very subtle and we can go from day to day without realising that we haven't done a thing towards our goals.

If you find yourself in this place as I have done in the past then let the alarm bells ring. That way we can focus once again on the journey that lies ahead. We must train ourselves not to take our foot off the pedal until we have arrived. Of course, you and I both know that there will be times when you need to step back a little and re-evaluate your course. But we must make sure that we don't pull off the side of the road for a nap in the sleepy hollow of life and fail to get back on the road once we have rested.

What will seem difficult in the beginning becomes habit over time. The daily disciplines that you develop will in time come as naturally to you as eating, sleeping and breathing. The day you set upon a goal with true commitment to yourself and your dreams you become stronger. The *Universal Laws* tell us that we will become stronger in every area of our lives. Your health literally improves overnight. Spiritually you feel better. Your energy levels are increased as you begin pursuing something that is worthwhile and meaningful to you.

I had the experience of working in a job I would rather have not been in. I was turning up for work and I felt like an old ox with a yoke around my neck. The lack of fulfilment was weighing on me heavily to the point where it was affecting my relationships with family and friends. My health began to suffer. Subconsciously I would create an illness so I could get the sufficient time off until I could re-charge my emotional battery again. Once I gathered my strength I went straight back to the source that was dragging me down. I felt out of control. By not taking action on the dream that I truly desired I felt as though every day was taking me further away from it. The hourglass of lost time was slowly running out. This experience holds a valuable lesson. This is one of the greatest lessons in life that I am about to share with you.

The ability to stay true to yourself regardless of circumstances is one of the toughest stands that you will probably ever take. It takes courage to act boldly when society is pressuring you to do what's right by their standards. Many people will never understand what it is you are creating for yourself. We each hold the dream inside us and yet the failure to act on our dreams is one thing that can chain us down. What do we do about it?

Now that you have come this far you will have already realised that there is so much you could have already done in the past without having completed the exercises laid out in this book. This is the case with every single person I have met.

As humans we can each think of at least a few things that we could have done to get the ball rolling long before this book was ever opened. The purpose of mentioning action in this context is that there is always something that you can do to move you in the direction of your dreams.

You now have a good long list of goals that you will continue to add to. You have clear values and priorities that will guide you and give you the courage to take that stand when choices distract you. The people who master *The Power of Subconscious Goal Setting* are all great exponents of action. If something needs to be done they get right to it.

It's Action Time

Throughout this book I have normally placed exercises for you to complete towards the end of a chapter. You can treat this as a little test for yourself. I mentioned earlier the importance of completing exercises that fit with your highest priorities right away. You must not develop the habit of coming back to it later. This is just developing the habit of putting things off. We refer to this habit as procrastination.

Right NOW I want you to go to your plan and make a list of all the things you can do *starting today* that will move you closer to the realisation of your goals. As you develop this list you will begin to notice just how much you have been putting off in the past. Add to the list you already have from the exercise on planning.

Begin by writing down the things you could have done before you read this book. Maintain your momentum. Do not strive for perfection because it doesn't exist. Just become excellent at what you do and the rest will take care of itself.

Anything you write down that you feel is outside of your capabilities will be tasks that you either develop the skills to do, or find someone who can do it for you. Go ahead and add to your list right now. It only has to be a few tasks. It's the habit of taking action when you think of something that will move you in the direction of your dreams. The little things add up to a huge amount in a very short period of time. If you don't believe me try putting $3 in a jar every day for a few years. You will be a wealthy person.

What are you waiting for?

Consider yourself a disciplined achiever destined for great things if you add to your list right now. I promise I will wait for your return right here.

ACTION steps you should have taken by this point in the book.

- Responsibility - Your identity list
- Values - Your list of values, defined and prioritised
- Goals - 101 Goal List, *Perfect Day*, Category of Goals (prioritised)
- Planning - Answer the areas in your plan and take some action.
- Beliefs - Create a list of quotes you can review to shape your beliefs.
- Action - This is what you can do NOW! Phone someone, write something, draw something, buy something, borrow something, read something, enrol in a course, enter an event, make an appointment to speak with an expert, etc.

Signpost That Tells All

The actions that you engage in on a consistent basis tell you a great deal about yourself. It is said that procrastination on a particular task is a sign that you don't really believe. You either don't believe you can achieve the end result or you don't believe you can comfortably complete the task at hand. You subconsciously put it off in order to protect yourself from going outside your *Circle of Comfort*.

The key is to recognise your procrastination and overcome your own self-doubt by pushing through the self-imposed *Road Blocks* you have. The unknown carries with it one of the greatest of human fears. There is the story of a man who was trapped by the enemy and given a choice. The choice was to be stoned and risk death or to walk through a door marked 'Unknown'. The man's fear of the unknown led him to the decision to face his own death by choice. He did not survive the stoning. After the incident was over a young women asked the General what was behind this mysterious door. The general replied, "*Freedom, but no one has ever walked through it*".

The next time you are faced with your own fears choose to walk forward. The door to freedom awaits you but no one can walk through it for you. You must be willing to turn the key to your better future yourself. You must step into the unknown. The wonderful thing about it is that whenever we take this leap of faith we find that it is never really as bad as we first imagined. With each step into the unknown we become more and more confident. We eventually reach a point where we look behind us and wonder what we were uncomfortable about in the first place. Never conform to your *Circle of Comfort* when you can take action and cause your *Circle of Comfort* to adjust to you.

Every mental signpost you read that says, 'Fear of the Unknown' or 'Uncomfortable road ahead' is best interpreted as a sign that reads **'Take action now!'** The more often you take action the less these feelings of discomfort and fear tend to arise. Your journey begins to smooth out as you overcome your own procrastination and doubts and move forward into freedom and personal fulfilment. The greater the success you are aiming for the bigger these negative signs will seem. Like a hazy mirage on the highway ahead, it disappears as you move closer. What was a figment of your imagination is easily overcome by continuing on. If you will take action on a daily basis, you will arrive at a destination beyond what you first dreamed and your life will never be the same.

Get Your Hands Dirty

Do you know of people who have been literally handed some amazing opportunities in life that have failed to take advantage of them because they were not prepared to get down and dirty? Rob Pearse is a friend and colleague who once said to me, *"If you're digging for gold, you've got to go through the dirt first"*.

You must be prepared to do what it takes. Many people look to those who have arrived and only see the nice cars and the nice houses. They fail to realise that these people went through an enormous amount of hard work and sacrifice.

The movie *Shawshank Redemption* tells the story of a man named Andy Dufresne who was innocently jailed for a crime he did not commit. He spent years upon years digging his way through concrete with a teaspoon. Every day he would empty a small handful of dirt into the exercise yard. The tunnel he created emerged at the beginning of a one and a half mile swim through sewerage in order to reach freedom. Andy was prepared to do what it takes. Andy Dufresne is now free. What are you prepared to do to be free?

The hardest work one can engage in is their personal development. To become successful requires an attitude of *"I will do whatever it takes"*. The rewards will be worth it. Once we begin to understand that each sacrifice carries with it the seed to a greater benefit we will do just about anything.

We were each given the ability to succeed. The desire we feel for our dreams and goals is an expression of our potential. It begins with the seed of thought and when acted upon will eventually and inevitably become the reality we desire. It is only if we fail to carry out the necessary actions that our seeds begin to rot in the ground of excuses.

Mortal Enemy of Action

When driving a car you eventually come to a point where you will visibly see a STOP sign. You know within yourself that it won't be long before someone pulls up behind you and gives you the hurry up if you don't move along. The road to success is different. You can sit there with your foot on the brake forever unless you give yourself the hurry up you need. The irony is that in life some people are sitting there staring at green lights with their foot on the brake. Many people believe their life has stalled when really they just need to shift themselves into gear and put the pedal to the metal. Very few of us have someone behind us that will continually honk the horn if we sit still too long.

Procrastination is sitting there, staring at the green light and refusing to take our foot off the brake. Many of these same people will also arrive at the end of their life only to find they have barely lived within a fraction of their potential because they couldn't bring themselves to do that little bit each day that brings the greatest rewards. They will continue to engage in the same monotonous tasks that they dislike, go to jobs that they dislike and even stay in a marriage with someone they dislike. The fear of taking a step back so they can detour and get on the fast track is too much work for some people. They are happier just to stay in their *Circle of Comfort* of second gear and chug along.

Newsflash for Procrastinators - everyone starts off in first gear at the beginning of a great race. Second newsflash - you can never hit top gear whilst you have one foot on the brake.

The people who are failing in this world try to excuse their procrastination with comments such as *"I'll wait and see how things work out"* or *"tomorrow is another day"*.

> **"Procrastination is death on a time payment plan."**
> **- Sheila Murray Bethel**

Og Mandino said, "Tomorrow can only be found on the calendar of fools". We all know that tomorrow never comes.

In order to live the life you have imagined you must do what you can with what you have right now. The wisdom of Benjamin Franklin has never rang so true as when he said, *"Never put off till tomorrow, that which you can do today"*.

Each of us can do something right now that will move us closer to the achievement of our goals. I know I am repeating myself but it's true that with every minute that passes something else pops into your mind that could be acted upon.

To achieve your goals and dreams, you need to look at how it is you are spending your days? If not invested wisely, time can become the biggest expense you ever make. If you think the lack of money hurts, let me remind you of the story of a millionaire who was left lying on his deathbed just wishing he had spent more time at home with his family.

"No success in life can compensate for failure in the home."
- Benjamin Disraeli

Regardless of your life's passion or what you value most, you owe it to yourself to invest your time into that which you love. Do not squander it on the tasks that leave you stagnating in the swamp of your own regret. I hope I said that well so that it sticks in your mind so you always remember it. Procrastination really is nothing more than death on a time-payment-plan. Every minute wasted is one less minute of fulfilment you will get to experience in your life. The clock is ticking. To live every day as though it was our last is what a successful happy life is all about. The mortal enemy of procrastination suffocates under the daily actions toward your dream.

"Stop acting as though you have a thousand years to live."
- Marcus Aurelius (121-180AD)
Roman Emperor and Philosopher

Convenience Disease

As the world has become more technologically advanced we are faced with a disease of convenience that if not immunised against can kill our future. Convenience is plaguing the futures of more people than ever before in history. Whilst it has its advantages when it comes to tiresome duties, it is also simultaneously creating habits of laziness that can doom the fulfilment of goals.

This convenience disease where we each seek the fastest and easiest ways to do things has created a mentality in society of the 'get rich quick' thinking which promotes wealth with misinterpreted minimal effort. It is not to say that people don't create an extraordinary amount of money in short periods of time. The fallacy in society is that it is done with minimal work, minimal effort and minimal thoughts and actions.

The abundance of money, health and relationships you attract is always in proportion to the thoughts and actions you engage in. It is a *Universal Law*. The answers are there. See if you can recognise what's missing in the people I talk about below.

In 2002 in this little country called Australia people squandered over $13.8 billion dollars which equates to an average of $980 per person for the year on gambling. The amount of money invested in lotto's and gambling in the hope of a windfall is staggering. I know of very small establishments that are based in very small towns that pull in over a million dollars a week in revenue through their gaming. To put one's hard earned money into these wishing wells in the hope of changing their lives is merely a reflection of one's consciousness. It sends a strong signal that the convenience disease is within. People who suffer from the convenience disease are missing what? They are missing a basic understanding of the *Universal Laws*.

The truth of the matter is that the fastest and easiest way to wealth, health and happiness is by engaging in the actions of those who are succeeding. You can take chances your whole life or you can knuckle down to the necessary tasks at hand. The trouble is that most people want the rewards without the effort. Make the effort.

You probably know someone who has gone to their boss asking for a pay rise only to be turned down because they weren't prepared to prove themselves first. They have the attitude of 'Give me the pay rise and then I'll go the extra mile for you'.

The effort is nothing compared to the reward but many people are simply not willing to make the effort in the first place. They are stuck in a rut that is so comfortable they dare not ruffle the pillow of security.

"There are no traffic jams when you go the extra mile."

To be successful you must immunise yourself against this convenience disease. This is where your freedom lies. If you are prepared to go down that extra mile soon you find yourself miles in front of the field.

The one hour of reading each day translates into a book a week. One book a week translates into fifty books a year. In a world where the average person reads less than three books when they leave high school, you can see that it doesn't take long before you stand apart.

Remember that success is looking for a good place to stay. Let's use money as an example. If you take good care of money you will notice that more of it will accumulate in your life. If you treat money badly how can you ever expect large sums of money to trust you with their future? Think about how you would treat your money if you had a savings account with $100,000 in it. If you had the responsibility to turn that money into more money could you be trusted with it? Some people make the excuse, *"I don't even have $50 to my name so what difference does it make"*. I think they are still missing the point. To become wealthy you must become the type of person that money feels comfortable being around. Someone that money can trust.

Action is all about taking the daily disciplines and having the faith to know that although the tasks may seem small and insignificant on their own, accumulated they are like the snowball rolling down the mountain. Each step of the way gathers momentum that eventually becomes an avalanche of abundance.

This is what taking action will do for you. Trust in its ability to accumulate. Have faith that each daily action carries a brick to the building of a great monument.

"Faith without action is dead."

Hard and Necessary

If you review your list of action steps that are contained in your plan you will find that some tasks have the ability to move you further and faster towards your goals than others. Take a minute to divide your list into the hard and necessary (one list), and the fun and easy (a second list). Invariably you will find it is the tasks which are hard and necessary that contain within them the most value.

In time management we often analyse someone's list of things to do and they will admit to starting on the easiest tasks first when they know that other things are more important.

One of the keys to achieving your goals is to discipline yourself to work single-mindedly on the tasks that contain the most value. We all like to think we are working when we engage in the easy tasks. But at the end of the day you will find the energy and thrill of achievement only come when you complete tasks of significance. The things that have the power to create an impact. That's how massive progress can be made in short periods of time.

Let me just point out that we do not want to engage in the hard tasks just for the sake of them. If you were putting an in-ground pool in your back yard you wouldn't dig the hole by hand just because Scott said we should resist taking the fastest and easiest way. The sensible thing would be to bring in a backhoe that could dig it out in a matter of hours. The point I am making is that we must not neglect the disciplines that create the magic. There will be certain ideas that only you are capable of bringing into reality because you are the one with the vision.

5 REASONS WHY PEOPLE FAIL TO FOLLOW THROUGH.

It is time to take a look at the five major reasons why it is people fail to follow through on their own desires. (And what to do about them)

1. Lack of Congruency with our Highest Values

The truth of the matter is that action should be the automatic effect of having congruent values. In the chapter on values and beliefs I mentioned that all decisions and actions are the result of what you value and believe. If you truly do value your dreams and goals, then taking action towards the fulfilment of them should be automatic. If you find yourself wilting over any period of time then I would recommend that you look over your list of values to refresh your memory. If you followed my advice from the values section you would already have a list made out that you carry with you wherever you may go.

Keep a list on the bathroom mirror where you get ready in the morning. This way you can get your day started with the focus not just on your goals but also on the principles which you stand for and the things that are most important in your life.

2. Lack of Patience

Patience is a virtue. I'm sure you've all heard that one before. It is now considered a virtue more than ever. In the fast paced world we live in today it is becoming easier to get things when we want. Impatience is deciding we want something then demanding we had it yesterday. Just for a second, try to imagine yourself, operating from this perspective 2000 years ago as you were farming your own crop of vegetables. You place the seeds in the ground. You cover them up and give them some water. And you stand there waiting for them to leap out of the ground at you and jump in your hand made bucket. You stand there impatiently tapping your foot as the first few minutes pass by. You snidely look at the sundial on your wrist as your blood begins to curdle with impatience.

Many people demand things now. It is the convenient disease at work once again. The danger of impatience is obvious. However the rewards of patience can take your breath away. Just stop for a moment and think of all the great things in the world that there are to admire. Think of the great buildings in Rome, the wonderful Pyramids in Egypt, the unique Mona Lisa. It is rare that you will find something of great beauty that came about instantly. A great life must also be crafted. You are the draftsperson and engineer of your own life. The bigger, better and more beautiful you want something to be the more patient you will need to become.

Practice the *Law of Gender* for you cannot rush a gestation period. A foetus takes nine months before a beautiful baby can be held. Good things take time. Be patient.

3. Lack of Discipline

Why do people lack discipline? Discipline is really just a habit.

Once while eating lunch with a friend named Sharyn Campbell, she commented on me pulling the skin off my chicken and said, "*You are so disciplined*". I thought about that comment later on and came to the realisation that I'm not disciplined with chicken skin at all. I have simply developed the habit of doing it. I don't give it any conscious thought at all.

The reason that people lack discipline is because they have habits that don't support the goals they are trying to reach. This is why people fight and struggle with themselves in order to override their previous conditioning. Real discipline forms the development of habit. Rather than trying to become disciplined, I find it much more supportive in the long run to focus on developing a habit that supports what I want to achieve. Discipline is only required to develop the habit. After that, it comes automatically.

The only danger with a lack of discipline is that we never permanently develop the habits that allow us to continue our actions with any consistency. The performance over time becomes an up and down rollercoaster. The consequences for most people on this rollercoaster are the ranges of emotions and financial ups and downs that go with the territory. The lack of discipline ultimately causes more heartache and feelings of insecurity than any other characteristic we may possess.

Whenever you are not happy with your performance you can always trace it back to discipline. The solution is to develop a habit that is going to transport you to where it is you want to go.

4. Lack of Action

One of the things I have developed to give greater understanding to what motivates people is a *'Motivation Model'*. I hear many people comment on their wishes and dreams and then finish the sentence with, *"but I just can't get myself motivated to do anything about it"*. Have you heard this one from anyone you know?

A lot of people get things the wrong way around when it comes to motivation and what gets us to take action on a consistent basis. Lack of action is the cornerstone of failure, whilst action is the cornerstone of success. You can think positive until the cows come home, but if you fail to take any positive actions then you will remain bound to your previous existence.

Success is simply a matter of applying what you know. This book is a formula for success. If you follow the steps laid out in it then you can have what you desire. If you falter on some of the steps then each act of doing less than your best will detract from the end result. It's not rocket science. Success is simple. That's why it doesn't take a genius to achieve great things. There are many stories of people leaving high school and achieving incredible results; living lives that most only dream about. Although these same people left school with a 'C' grade average they've discovered the secret to action.

The Motivation Model best sums up why people do what they do or why they fail to do it. You will see how this model ties in to the whole process we are discussing in *The Power of Subconscious Goal Setting*.

The greater the understanding you have, the easier it will be for you to implement your ideas. And if you do get stuck, the easier it is to identify the true causes and how to move past it.

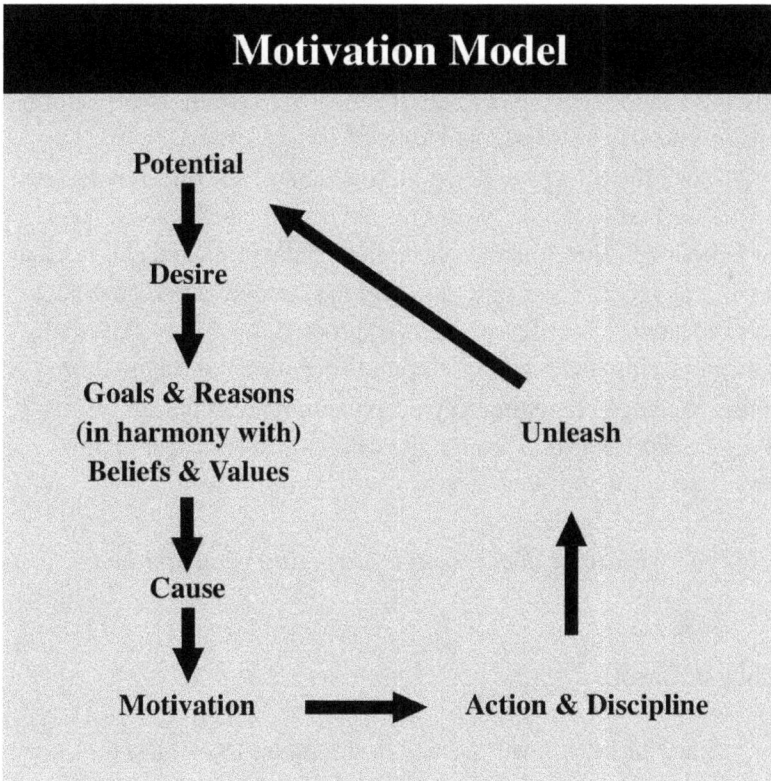

Motivation Model

Potential

↓

Desire

↓

**Goals & Reasons
(in harmony with)
Beliefs & Values**   **Unleash**

↓

Cause

↓

Motivation ➡ **Action & Discipline**

This *Motivation Model* explains the simple cause effect relationship that exists. When someone tells you that they are not motivated it is due to their lack of goals. They experience a lack of goals because they choose to ignore the desires that their potential is trying to express through them.

"Desire is your potential talking to you." - Scott Groves

Once people recognise their desires as an indicator of their potential they begin to develop belief in their goals. The congruency that comes from having your goals aligned with your values and beliefs will cause motivation like you've never felt before. Motivation moves you into action. It provides you with energy and drive to be disciplined. The actions work to reinforce your ability and belief in yourself. This is what will unleash your pure potential. The Motivation Model becomes a self-feeding mechanism. Every action intensifies desire, instilling the habits of action further.

Take the time to understand this model. For once understood, you will see that each goal you set influences the beliefs you have. Your beliefs will develop and create new behaviours and actions that you will engage in. Over time you literally become a person who is acting in an entirely different manner, producing entirely different results and living an entirely different life. And all of this will be because you began listening to your potential that is naturally seeking to express itself through the desires you feel. Gut instinct comes from acting on your feelings.

"If you wish to be successful, try applying what you know."

5. Lack of Faith

Faith has the power to take desire and inject it into the subconscious mind for the development of potential. Every religion of the world speaks of the power of faith. I like faith because anyone can relate to it. You don't have to believe in a particular religion for faith to work for you. Faith is universal in its presence. Faith is what you call on when your vision temporarily vanishes. In the bible it says,

"Faith calls forth those things that are not, as though they were."

This is one of the best definitions of faith that I have heard. It is about believing when there is no evidence to support that belief.

There are times along the pursuit of our dreams that we can become discouraged or lose our way. The heart can grow weary with constant striving. Without physical evidence we know only through faith the progress we have made. Patience is waiting for goals to materialise. Faith knows your goals will. Doubts and fears can walk in and out of your life but they are only temporary visitors when faith is guarding the door.

This fifth reason why people fail to follow through is critical. You don't have to be religious to believe in faith. Faith is about certainty, knowing and believing that someday, somehow you'll make it and everything will be alright. There's a quotation I'd like you to remember with regards to faith.

**"Where there is no faith in the future,
there is no work in the present."**

Make the daily practice of believing in your goal with the faith that you will arrive; regardless of what physical appearances may tell you.

4 WAYS TO STOP THE LACK OF ACTION

You have probably already made some decisions about how to overcome these five reasons that doom under achievers. They are simply overcome with the right approach. Many of which have been discussed throughout this book so far. As you can appreciate, mastering each of these individual areas will take time. Repetition being the mother of skill, this section is to serve as a reminder. You can refer back here if you catch yourself drifting off course with your goals.

There are three characteristics or habits that you will develop as a result of sticking to the action plans in this book. I have chosen to bring them to your conscious awareness here. These are what will prevent you from becoming a victim of the 5 reasons why people fail to follow through.

1. Awareness

Awareness lets you know how things are travelling. Awareness of yourself and the way you're feeling. Are you charging ahead or holding yourself back? The ability to relax at the right time and to also take the necessary breaks will ultimately be determined by your awareness. Awareness keeps your mind fresh and alert.

With regular revision of your goals you will develop the focus and intuition to know that you are on the right track. Your subconscious will guide you and direct you with feelings of righteousness. *"Yes this feels right"* or *"No this doesn't feel right"*, will be easy to recognise with practice. Awareness is what will recognise desire for what it is. This awareness is what will cause you to act on those desires. Awareness is therefore the basis to all action.

2. Concentration & Focus

Concentration and focus are two different beasts that work together in a harmonious way. Concentration moves through time. It's like getting absorbed in a single activity for 2 hours. Time stands still. Things appear to slow down whilst you move deeply inside productive action.

Focus is a single focal point. Like a target on a tennis court. Or an end goal. Focus stands still. It zeros in on a single object, single point in time.

Another way of saying this in relation to goals is concentration is the journey, the goal is the focus.

Your ability to focus and pull yourself up in the moment on negative thoughts or mental holidays helps maintain concentration throughout the course of the day. Action requires concentration so your actions lead to efficient and effective results. It is pointless to take a lot of action and fail to pay attention. You may end up having to do something all over again. So pay attention. Keep your mind in the here and now. Maximise the use of your time so that your time is not being consumed by things that pop up out of the ordinary.

Concentration is one of the key characteristics to time management. This is where great strides are made.

"Concentration creates compound progress."

In my coaching days I used to have people stare at a tennis ball to develop their concentration muscle. It is something that is initially very challenging. With practice we found some students spending up to fifteen minutes in deep concentration. Do you think this helped improve their tennis? You bet it did. Knowing they could go the distance in a long rally without diversion or distraction can make all the difference.

Distraction is one of your greatest enemies in the digital age. But if we are being really honest, most of them are self-imposed. Too many apps, too many notifications. Email open all the time with reminders up the wazoo. If this was someone ringing your door bell every few minutes, you'd punch them in the face. Stop doing this to yourself. To achieve great things requires deep work. You don't slip into concentration in seconds. Every distraction sets you back at least 30 minutes according to the latest science. The path to success in any endeavour is going deep.

It is the same for you with your goals. How long can you hold the picture in your mind of what you want to achieve? Your ability to keep your eyes on your goal without distractions is critical to your ability to follow through. Concentration intensifies action and gets you in the zone. Create that tunnel vision that all successful people can call up at will.

3. Daily

Do something that takes you closer to your goal every single day. If you rest too long you will lose focus and find yourself wasting valuable time trying to work out where you were up to and what needs to be done next. Following through is all about consistency. Consistently take concentrated action with faith and patience. Consistently act in accordance with your highest payoff tasks (values) and do it with discipline and awareness as your allies.

There is no one on this planet that couldn't follow through with a formula for success like this. It is only a matter of giving yourself and your goals the attention they deserve on a daily basis. Success is no accident and there is no such thing as an overnight success. Wealth is no accident and there is no such thing as an overnight millionaire. Although you'll hear the claims in newspapers and in magazines, it is the journalists and public who are wishing and dreaming of a pot of gold that doesn't exist that continue to tell these stories. No one ever sees the work and preparation that goes into the success one creates. You can sit there right in front of your closest friends and family writing out your goals. The day you put the last dollar in that million dollar account they will still think that it's happened practically overnight.

I am not saying that wealth and success cannot be created within short periods of time. One year is not an overnight success. The preparation that is required to make a million dollars is achieved in the shortest periods of time by those with the sharpest vision. They do the most preparation in the shortest period of time. They work to create with greater concentration than the average person. It is all relative. You cannot shortcut one million dollars. It is counted the same in all countries. The difference is how one gets there.

Daily action is the only reliable path. Daily action will compound you towards your goals. It makes use of these natural Universal Laws. You know WHAT you want. You know WHY you want it. You even know HOW. Ignorance can no longer be the excuse when we know how. Taking action is acknowledging your desires.

"Wisdom comes from doing."

4. Streaks

Jerry Seinfeld is probably the most successful comedian in the history of the world. He started out like any other comedian. Late nights working clubs. Hold down another job during the day. Somehow find time to work on your craft in between. It's a story anyone can relate to.

Comedians work in "bits". Every joke is a "bit". And a comedians ability to get it right, remember it and deliver it in the way that has proven to get the best audience reaction is one of the great secrets of comedians. Except it's not secret. It's hard work.

The concept of the TV show Seinfeld was a game changer for Jerry. It put him on the map like no other comedian has ever experienced.

Backstage one night, a young software developer named Brad Isaac who was dabbling in comedy approached Jerry for some advice on how to be a better comedian.

Jerry explained to Brad that every January, he would hang a large yearly planner on his wall. Every day that he wrote new material, he would take joy in putting a red 'X' over that day. Soon enough, a long chain of red 'X's would appear all strung together.

His advice to Brad, "Don't break the chain".

In the Netflix documentary, "Jerry Before Seinfeld" you see Jerry sitting in the middle of the road, surrounded by every single "bit" of paper he has ever written. Jerry looks around and says, "Every time I wrote something that worked, I saved it in this accordion folder. Every single thing. And this is it, from 1975 until this morning."

A streak is when you string together consecutive days of action. It's that simple.

"Action creates traction. Traction creates attraction."
- Roger Hamilton

I believe the #1 reason people get good at something is a "Streak". If you really stop and think about it, what else could it be. You need to practice. You need regular action. You need to be consistent.

If you want healthy teeth, you brush them every day. If you want to be lean and healthy, you simply eat clean every day. If you want to build legs that can run a marathon you run consistently. More days than you don't.

Here's a good opportunity to discuss the finer points of streaking. Some streaks are best done every day. Some are not!

I have friends who run every single day. Whilst it might sound impressive and even look good in a Guinness Book of Records somewhere - as a high performance practice, it's plain dumb. The physical body will only ever achieve truly high performance when 'rest' is treated as training. Rest is a very important part of getting in peak condition. In business, you can't work every single day of the year without taking a holiday - and you shouldn't.

With physical transformations and achieving goals like Marathon personal bests, etc - it will only happen with the right consistency and rest combined. You still have streaks. But very smart, strategic streaks that lead you naturally to the best results.

Want to stop drinking alcohol? Give up sugar? Drink more water? These are best as a 7 day a week streak. But with some goals, you might choose to spread your actions into a 5 day a week, or 6 day a week streak. Your goal then becomes to string together consecutive weeks of 6 days a week for 48 weeks of the year. Be clear about your action plan up front.

Want to learn to code? Code Monday to Saturday for at least one hour. Be a better salesperson? Present to someone every day, 5 days a week. And if you are struggling to make that happen, you need to do prospecting and marketing 5 to 6 days a week. Want to learn guitar? You get the idea!

No matter what you want to change for yourself in life, if you just applied yourself with consistency - built a streak, you find almost nothing becomes impossible.

Points to Remember on Action

1. Action is the essential element that will keep your goals alive.

2. Procrastination is a signpost of disbelief.

3. Get your hands dirty.

4. If there's hard work to be done then work it hard.

5. Avoid the 5 reasons why people fail to follow through.

6. *Motivation Model* - cause and effect of motivation.

7. Faith is the certainty to know you'll succeed.

8. Concentrate to compound the effect of action.

9. You must GO TO work on your goals. Nothing happens until you DO something.

10. Daily actions create the snowball of momentum.

"Success is the accumulation of little things done in a great way on a regular basis." - Scott Groves

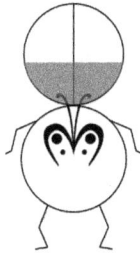

CHAPTER 8

Self Talk

The way you communicate with yourself is critical to your success. There are basically three ways we communicate with ourselves. One way is questioning and the second is the statements or affirmations we say to ourselves. The third way in which we unconsciously communicate to ourselves is developed through habit. I like to call it our "*Inner Conversation*".

Over time we have each developed this *Inner Conversation* that directs our behaviour without us even knowing. We sometimes catch the voice of it in our conscious awareness as the *Inner Conversation* works to talk us out of the things we want the most. Since we live in a predominantly negative world where disaster dominates the headlines, it is no surprise to find that the majority of peoples self-talk is negative. Most of the people you come across can come up with ten reasons why it *can't* be done before they can come up with two reasons why it can be done. Ask someone what they did wrong and most people don't even have to stop and think about it. Ask them what they did *right* and you will find that most people weren't even expecting the question. People are far more familiar with their *Inner Conversation* expressing the voice of doubt, mistakes and impossibility.

The *Inner Conversation* is programmed by the way we talk to ourselves and our subconscious answering to the questions we ask. When it becomes positively programmed, your *Inner Conversation* will act as your cheerleader encouraging you to fight on. That little voice inside your head will be saying, *"Come on, you can do this."*

Who Are You Answering To?

We basically communicate to ourselves through questioning. The challenge is we often are not consciously aware of what we are asking. But no matter what it is we ask, our subconscious will answer. If you ask yourself, *"why am I so stupid?"* Your brain will automatically go into overdrive and come up with an answer. Your subconscious will list enough reasons to satisfy your question. Answers that confirm exactly why you are so stupid.

On the flipside to this we can ask ourselves why we are so wonderful and we will also answer ourselves. The questions we ask ourselves lead to the statements we also use. A lot of people talk about the power of affirmations which is giving powerful, positive statements to our subconscious. The repetition of these statements eventually leads to the subconscious accepting the statements and then acting in a manner consistent with the new programming.

Wouldn't it be far easier to ask a question and let the subconscious answer it for itself? A golden rule in selling we teach is that you have to say something five times for a customer to believe you. But if we ask questions and the customer says it once then they believe it for themselves. Surely the same must apply with the way we communicate with ourselves.

Every time we ask a question, our *Inner Conversation* answers. Therefore success must lie in continually asking ourselves the right questions in order to elicit the right response. Play with this example for a minute and notice how you feel inside.

Firstly ask yourself the following question 10 times, *"Why do terrible things always happen to me?"* If you persist in asking this it won't take very long before your mind will begin to process answers and create the fact. Keep asking and very soon you will begin to feel miserable.

When you have had enough of this try asking yourself, *"Why do great things keep happening to me? What is it I have to be grateful for? What did I do right?"* Notice the different way you begin to feel. Your subconscious begins to vibrate on a totally different plane of thought. It resonates with more energy and you begin to feel more alive.

Never ever ask yourself what you did wrong. This serves absolutely no useful purpose. This question will inevitably program your subconscious to continue repeating the negatives, as that is all it can recall. Charge your mind with every single good thing you can muster up. What's the best way for me to achieve my goals and have fun doing it? Just think about the type of answers that this question will stimulate.

It is when we are down that our *Inner Conversation* has a tendency to question our worth and capabilities. It is in these moments that people try to conjure up the resilience to stay positive and force themselves into a state that doesn't seem to fit. The truth of the matter is that it requires no more willpower to be successful than it does to be a failure. In fact, thoughts that resonate on a higher vibration actually create more energy from which you can operate.

The confusion comes when people are forcing themselves to act without thinking. They are in a state of low energy with their mind dominated by negative thoughts and thinking positive is simply too much of a stretch at the time. If you have ever been a bit down and you've had someone console you and tell you to "Be positive" you have probably felt the inner resistance I am talking about.

My point is this, you don't have to answer the questions, just ask them. Let your subconscious answer them. All you have to do is stop asking questions that bring about negative answers and ask questions that bring about positive answers. It takes the same amount of effort to ask a positive question as it does a negative question. If you are not ready, don't answer them, but keep on asking them and you won't be fighting yourself by trying to force yourself into as positive state. Let it happen. No one wants to wallow in feelings of depression or sadness. But at the same time, we don't want to make the effort to drag ourselves into a genuine smile. It is all a matter of taking the right approach. Questions provide the answers. Ask them and then get out of the way.

The Power of 'Why'

Why questions are what Anthony Robbins refers to as *"Endless Loop"* questions. They never end. Children are the masters of the 'why' question. It's almost as if they were born with this knowledge that it never ends and this is all you have to say to get anything you want. It works on ice-creams, chocolate, you name it. As a child I don't remember having classes on the subject of 'why' but I seemed to do pretty well when I used it.

It is these questions that lead us into the future. The purpose of bringing this type of communication to our level of awareness is to prepare ourselves so that we are no longer the victim of circumstance, but rather the master of it. In the seminars we run I often say that, *"Negative circumstances are simply experiences that we have not emotionally mastered yet"*. When we master our ability to respond, we pause just long enough to ask ourselves the type of questions that will draw the positive out of every situation. I am not saying that some circumstances aren't pleasant. Some circumstances are totally unpleasant, but when we control our communication with ourselves, we control our own personal worlds.

'Why' questions are neutral. They can be used both positively and negatively. If you ask yourself, "Why did this happen to me?" after a negative circumstance, you will find a list of negative reasons that can plague you for days if not months after the event. If after a positive experience you asked the same question you will probably come up with a sound list of reasons as to why you succeeded.

Although I am a fan of the question 'why' I am very wary of how I use it when communicating with myself. I use it only in the section on goals when I am developing a list of reasons as to 'why' I want to achieve a particular goal. I tend to avoid it for the most part because of its nature to continually persist. With most of our day to day self-talk I recommend using questions like the ones I have listed below. They give you sharp focus and keep your mind in the here and now.

- What have I done today that has moved me closer to achieving my goals?
- What did I do right today?
- What could I do to improve on what I did today?
- What is it I will do tomorrow that will move me even closer to my goals?
- What is the best use of my time right now?
- Who else could help me achieve my goals?
- How did they do that? (Model someone you admire)

It's okay to be impressed by outstanding performances, but you should also learn from them when you can.

Use 'WHY' questions to build the emotional reasons for reaching your goals.

Use 'WHAT' questions to maintain sharp focus and create clarity.

AFFIRMATIONS

Affirmations are powerful commands that you input into the subconscious mind. However, they are often misinterpreted and incorrectly used. They are often corny, long winded spiels that bore the life out of people. The definition of affirmations means to confirm or support.

Allow me to share with you the 4 areas that we can use affirmations to support what we are trying to achieve.

WARNING: In order to successfully apply the ideas I am about to share will require a high degree of awareness on your part. Much of what goes on within us goes on without our conscious awareness. With regular use of these ideas your subconscious programming will change and you will begin to set goals in areas of your life that your mind couldn't previously comprehend. Are you ready?

Affirmation of Thought

Thought supports or confirms our subconscious conditioning more than any other element I will describe here. It does so both positively and negatively and it is almost as though it feeds upon itself. A negative mind has no problem in herding up negative thoughts to reinforce itself. As with the *Law of Belief* discussed earlier we have no trouble in finding evidence to support our current situation or circumstances when we are not thinking.

Thoughts race through our minds at a rapid rate. In as little as one minute we think at a rate of around 500 words, compared to our speech ability of around 100-200 words a minute. If you have ever tuned out in a conversation or lost concentration reading a book (someone else's book) you now know why.

What you think about is critical. What you let your *Inner Conversation* run away with is up to you. Many times driving my car I suddenly become aware of my train of thought drifting. I then have the decision to pull it up or play it out. Too often we can drive, metaphorically speaking for miles until we hit a dead end. We reach an empty well that is drained of ideas and inspiration. Can you relate to this type of thinking?

Here are a couple of tips you can use to influence your surroundings and ultimately your subconscious mind (*Inner Conversation*).

- Leave inspirational quotes or ideas lying around. I always have quotes or sayings on the dashboard of my car.

Note: Do not cover your Speedo or fuel gauge. (I will leave it up to your imagination how I learned that piece of wisdom - no laughing please)

- Write out some post it notes to yourself with questions on them to cause you to come up with positive answers. I have been known to distribute these around the house at various light switches and in cupboards where I regularly look. Back in my days in selling, I once used a good financial affirmation which bought in an extra $5,000 in commission within two weeks of sticking one up. (I'll tell you what it said in a minute)

- Buy a calendar with inspirational pictures of achievement and positive quotations.

- Use colours that enhance positive feelings. Red / Orange (confidence), Yellow (uplifting), Blue (tranquil). Avoid blacks and greys (boring!).

Affirmations of Actions

Each of us engages in actions that both support and confirm to us where we are at. A good example of affirmation of action would be someone who consistently procrastinates. Each act supports or influences the subconscious and we will continue to perform in a manner consistent with that act. Whilst many people talk about positive thinking, it is somehow not enough. We must affirm to ourselves through positive doing also.

"We are judged by our actions - not our intentions."

Another way to put this would be, *"Actions speak louder than words"*. We can all relate to the words we speak when talking about affirmations, but few of us stop to think about the effects that our actions are having. We must not confuse activity with action. It's easy to act like busy little beavers scurrying around as winter approaches. But if you're not gathering nuts you will starve to death.

Affirmations of Actions is all about doing things that get results. Results that will carry you closer to your goals. We talked enough about action in the last chapter so the purpose of recognising it as an affirmation is to make you see it in a different light. See it as something that has more of a contribution than just the result itself. It is a habit that is developed as a result that is important.

Affirmations of Feelings

The feelings we experience have the power to move us. The way you feel about something determines how vividly you remember it. The greater the feeling of the moment the more vividly we remember. Feelings have the greatest influence when it comes to the subconscious mind. Since affirmations are normally thought of as words we need to put into perspective their effect on feelings. Words describe feelings. It gives us the ability to explain a vibration or frequency we experience through labelling. Let me pose you with a philosophical question: Do feelings determine what words you use to describe a particular feeling or do the words you use determine how you feel?

What you will notice is that the words you use actually affect the way you feel. Your self-talk conjures emotional feelings and reinforces them with each repetition of that word.

I had an awkward experience with a sales team once where we were co-ordinating a joint territory to be worked by three different operations. The entire east coast of Australia was involved and it became an organised mess. Two adjacent states were entering into the territory of the third. As the communication broke down, it developed mixed feelings about how it would go amongst the teams.

What we were trying was new and there were many benefits to be derived from the cross pollination of ideas. The logistics proved to be a disaster. The foul taste it left in the mouths of some of the consultants from the home territory was like we had just asked them all to bite into a stale lemon and chew for a month.

I tried many ways to help our consultants get it off their chest yet I wasn't making any inroads. Finally we arrived at a regular quarterly meeting and some four weeks later there was still tension in the air. The experience I am about to share with you taught me a valuable lesson.

We began the meeting and things were not going smoothly. The tension was obvious so the Marketing Manager and I decided to give them another opportunity to clear the air.

It began like an out of control tornado as the comments and blame whirled around the room. Not being able to see where it would end I approached the whiteboard. In an attempt to gain some order in the room I asked them to give me a couple of words to describe the experience of this mini joint venture. What happened was quite incredible.

As we began going around the room, the difference in views of this experience was to this day something that I'll never forget. The first word to go up on the board was the word, *"Frustrating"*. As we went around to the next couple of people the diversity of the team showed through. Out of the next four or five people came two words I will never forget, *"Traumatic"* and *"Interesting"*. I stopped and thought "WOW". How can two people who have shared the same experience have vastly different feelings about this? The person who had labelled the event as traumatic was having a really difficult time in coping with it. Sales for this person had plummeted in the weeks that followed. Meanwhile the person who found it interesting had continued with the same consistency of sales he always had.

It became clear to me that the label we give to the experience actually becomes the experience. I never in my wildest dreams would have called this *traumatic* and I am not judging the person who did. I, like many others reserve the word traumatic for deaths, major injury and funerals. The different vocabulary this person used actually created an entirely different set of feelings. The experience was totally different based on the words that were used. The Affirmation of Feeling was being confirmed by the label that had been put on the experience. The person who found the event *'interesting'* was blissfully indifferent to it all and able to move on.

Now the point of this is not to say that one way or the other is the right way of handling the situation. There is no right or wrong way. It all comes back to what it is you want to do. The point is that we must become aware of how we are affirming our feelings. Because of the significance our feelings have in relation to our subconscious, we owe it to ourselves to develop an awareness of how we are wired.

Over time, each of us has developed a vocabulary of feelings and words that are linked together to form our experiences. If there is a certain type of feeling that you want to experience then you should use that word more often. Use it to describe how you feel when someone says, *"How are you today?"* Conversely if there is a feeling that you want to avoid then avoid using the word and over time the feeling will subside to the point where it is strange to experience it.

I have used this approach with the feeling *worry*. Worry never solves, heals or prevents anything. Its only purpose is to make matters worse. Worry is one of the most debilitating affirmations of feeling we can entertain. I made the decision a long time ago to kick worry out the door. It started the day I refused to use the word anymore. Over time (and it took months) I have mentally reached a point where I literally do not worry. I still have concerns but I refuse to let worry exist in my life. It has been a breakthrough for me. As a result my finances improved, my health improved and I became a more focused happy individual.

It's a good idea to make a list of the type of feelings you want to experience for the rest of your life and develop a list of words that make you feel that way. Can you imagine the difference something like this would mean to the outcomes of your goals and fulfilment in your life?

Affirmations of Words

There is little doubt that one thing leads to another in the process of goal setting. Just as responsibility affects our goals so does the power of words in many areas of our lives. Words have the ability to persuade, inspire, hurt, and bring joy. I could make a list as long as your arm with the many emotions there are. The point is their power can never be underestimated.

Words are the icing on the cake and the sweetness in the centre. They will be the link you need to a world where communication is vital. They are also the link to your own inner world where you create your own heaven or hell. The affirmations of words that you use with yourself and others will be the icing on your life. Express the way you feel about someone. Put it into words rather than have people die wondering.

Develop a generous vocabulary for yourself. Look upon yourself with kind eyes. We are always harder on ourselves than anyone else. One of your true tests of character is how to treat yourself when things aren't going your way. Be gentle with yourself. A kind word is the door to your own kindred spirit.

YOUR SUCCESS AND FAILURE DICTIONARY

Words to Avoid and Words to USE

Since we are now clearly aware of the amazing force our self-talk has on our subconscious it is time we develop the start of what will become your own personal *Success and Failure Dictionary*. I want you to be fully aware of the words you use on a regular basis. Look to eliminate words that program your subconscious for lack and limitation. Find words to replace them so you can experience freedom and abundance.

If you accidentally let the avoid words pop out of your mouth it's okay so long as you pull yourself up and mentally or verbally replace it immediately. It is about controlling your dominant thoughts.

Avoid: But Use: And

But should only ever be used when you want someone to disregard what you just said before it. For example, "*I used to think you were selfish **but** now I can see how kind hearted and generous you really are.*" The wrong way to use the word *'but'* which a lot of people do is, "*You look really pretty in that dress **but**...*" "*You are doing good work **but** there are a few areas I want to discuss with you.*" Gulp! You know you are in for it. A comment like this causes the defences to go up. It sends a strong signal that the person doesn't really believe you are doing good work because the *'but'* negates everything that is said prior to it.

If you want to say something that someone will remember then you need to use the word *'and'*. For example, "*You are doing good work **and** there are a few areas I want to discuss with you.*" This one word difference has a totally different feel to the entire conversation. How do we use *'but'* with ourselves?

It works on the same principle. If you want your subconscious to take you seriously with your goals then make sure that you use 'and' after you make a statement in relation to your goals. I have heard so many people say, *"I know I can achieve my goal **but** I just need these few things to happen to get there."* If you catch yourself with any sort of statement that resembles this then alarm bells should be going off. If you are serious about achieving your goals then you will pull yourself up and instantly replace it with one word. Look at the difference it makes to the statement. *"I know I can achieve my goal **and** I just need these few things to happen to get there."* Totally transformed. Just reading it feels different doesn't it?

Avoid: Can't Use: Can

Henry Ford said, *"That if you believe you can or if you believe you can't, either way you are right."*

It doesn't take a brain surgeon to realise that if you say it can't be done, then you won't be able to achieve what you want from life. When you say that something can't be done, you are merely verbalising your own belief system with regards to that subject. If you were to spend any length of time studying the subject in question you might find (like with nearly all successful endeavours) that plenty of people CAN do it, it's just that you don't know how.

Rather than walking around saying *"It can't be done"*, we should be honest and say, *"It can be done, I just don't know how."* *Can't* really means that you don't know how to or you simply don't want to. Remove the word *can't* and make a decision. Decide whether you want to achieve great success and you are prepared to find out how to, or simply let it go.

Why put yourself through the agony? The word can't conjures feelings of helplessness and being out of control. If can't was real it would mean there was nothing you could do about it. The fact of the matter is there is always something you can do about any situation.

As you believe in yourself more you will find that the word CAN becomes central to your vocabulary and your life. In the final analysis it comes down to what you want to do and whether or not you are ready to enjoy the rewards of who you become on your quest for greatness.

Don't Use this Wisely

This has to be one of the most misused words in the world. The incorrect use of the word *'don't'* causes more people to miss out on what they want than you may be able to fathom. As we go through this, just stop at any moment and think about how enormously misused it is.

The human brain has great difficulty in recognising the word *'don't'*. In most cases it fails to recognise the word don't altogether. The subconscious recognises keywords or key phrases. The first computers ever built were modelled on the human brain. And the human brain recognises *'keywords'*.

I remember a sales manager who used to say to his consultants, *"Don't forget to send your reports in each morning"*. The consultants' brains only heard *"Forget - send - reports-each - morning"*. *'Forget'* is a keyword. Once accepted by the subconscious it will do exactly what it was told.

I have seen marketing campaigns for products that say things like *"Don't forget to ask about our special"*. This could be costing these companies thousands if not millions of dollars. A far better approach would be to use the word in a way that will make people respond. Send them a letter that says, *"Don't open this envelope in the next 24 hours"*. Who could resist?

A football club from a small town was advertising for membership in desperate financial times. Their sign was about four metres squared and read, *"Don't let our fate be the same as (another extinct football club)"*. It's almost like asking for trouble.

I have heard tennis players say to themselves, *"Whatever you do, don't miss this serve"*.

Re-read any of the above sentences again and leave out the word *'don't'* and you will have a good idea as to the probable outcome.

You can use the word *'don't'* to your advantage and I want you to use these ideas so that you can monitor how you use it in relation to your goals and dreams. One effective advertisement that I came across in my research said, *"Don't buy a computer until you can answer these 3 questions."* This is clever because it's telling people what you want them to do which is purchase a computer. Another enticing one I saw read, *"Don't read this unless you want to make lots of money"*. Honestly who could resist something like that?

It's as if we as a human race rebel from the word *don't* and do the opposite just out of spite or curiosity. If you glance back at the sub-title I used to begin this section you will notice the words 'Use this wisely' as the keywords. Take the time to observe how you use the word *'don't'*. If you are clever, then you too can have someone take out the garbage for you. Oh wait... That's me!

~~Don't forget~~ Please remember:
the subconscious recognises KEYWORDS

Avoid: Hope Use: Know

Hope is a word that lacks confidence. Its deceptive nature is interesting though, because it provides you with a sense of comfort. Hope is a pleasant feeling but it lacks real punch. Punch that you will need to create the life you have imagined. *"I hope I reach my goal"* is a far cry from *"I know I'll reach my goal"*.

Imagine going to see an expert in any sort of field and they habitually use the word 'hope'. The hairdresser who says, "*I hope I can give you the hairstyle you want for your wedding*". The salesman who says, "*I hope you get some value out of this product*". The doctor who says, "*I hope we can find out what's causing all this pain*". Their lack of confidence is obvious.

When you are talking with people about your goals, have certainty and confidence. Have belief in your ability to get the job done. "*I know I can win this tournament. I know I have prepared well enough. I know I can overcome the difficulties along the way. I know the enormous benefit this book will bring to you if you use this information.*" Get the point?

Release your tendency to hope and grab on to something more solid. Knowing has power, certainty and focus. All successful people have these qualities and so do you. If you say it, you own it.

Avoid: If Use: When

If there was such a thing as a *Success Dictionary* I am sure that the definition of "*IF*" would read: uncertainty, doubtful, hesitant and probably not. "*IF*" takes up a lot of mental space with things that never eventuate like, "*If I don't get that bonus for Christmas then I just don't know what I'm going to do.*" You will be a Master at recognising the "*If... then*" statements from the chapter on beliefs and realise that these types of statements tend to create more harm than good.

"*IF*" is the most used word in the world when people talk about the lottery. They use it to represent the million to one chance they see themselves as. "*If I ever get rich I would...*" or "*If I could just find the right kind of guy for once*" or "*If I could just get one lucky break for a change.*"

"*When*" on the other hand implies certainty that something is going to happen. People who use the word "*when*" use it with conviction. I must point out that "*when*" can be used in a negative sense also. We have all heard people utterly convince themselves that something bad is going to happen and all of our efforts to point out that it is not inevitable fall on deaf ears as they repeat their self-fulfilling prophecy.

A good rule of thumb is this:

Use "when" on all positives and "if " on all negatives.

Avoid: Impossible Use: Possible

There is magic in knowing that something is possible. We can use this word freely and never question our own personal integrity as we know we are not lying to ourselves when we say *"It is possible that I can have the life I have always dreamed"*. It is not saying that it will be easy it is saying that the possibility exists. The word *possible* creates an opportunity mindset that begins to recognise ways in which it can move you toward your desired outcome.

Impossible is a little bit like the word *"can't"* in the sense that it leaves our fate in someone else's hands. Even the great Mission Impossible series and more recently the blockbuster movie starring Tom Cruise featured people that were paid to do the impossible. All great inventors and successes of our days are people who existed in the Top 1% of civilization. They became specialists at finding solutions to situations that to the untrained mind appear impossible.

Just imagine jumping into a time machine and going back 100 years to try and convince people of what life will be like for them in the next 100 years. People would think that you were out of your mind. People would line up around the block to tell you that what you are talking about is impossible.

With exponential technologies and the rapid rate of change, today this is only amplified even more.

Yet you and I both know that nothing will stop progress and if they could just see it in their minds they too could hold it in their hands.

Today is no different for you. What would appear impossible will be a reality soon. In just a few years from now the average yearly income will be getting close to six figures per annum just through inflation. Yet there are people who will forever believe that it is impossible for them to become a millionaire. It is becoming more common every year.

Become a believer and anything becomes possible. Believe in its possibility today instead of tomorrow.

"Impossible is a word from the dictionary of fools."
- Napoleon Bonaparte, 1769-1821,
French General

Avoid: Problem Use: Challenge or Opportunity

The word *'problem'* conjures up images of hardship and pain. I know of very few people who love problems. In fact I struggle to think of anyone who even likes them.

People like to rise to the challenge and they like to seize opportunities. We have positive feelings towards challenge and opportunity and negative feelings towards problems. People who are succeeding are solution oriented people who make a habit of turning their problems into challenges and rising to the occasion.

A close friend and fellow entrepreneur, Matt Adams and I were running a Sales Team in Queensland, Australia. We refused to let anyone use the word 'problem' in our sales meetings or around other consultants. It dragged other people down into the negative energy level of the problem person and quickly destroyed morale. We were constantly pulling people up until they developed the habit of using the words challenge and opportunity. Their sales went up almost in direct proportion to how often they used the word challenge. Who would have guessed?

Avoid: Someday and Get Specific

I have already made mention of that lonely island called, 'Someday I'll'. It is an island where dreams are laid to rest.

Many have used this common catchphrase from time to time. I have been guilty on many occasions. Like all of the other success words in this *Success Dictionary* it is our intention to prevent the use of them until they eventually fail to escape our mouths and ultimately won't enter our minds.

Being totally aware of what you specifically aim to achieve is how you overcome the use of 'someday'. When you are reviewing your goals regularly you will be more inclined to talk about the specifics of when you will be completed.

Being specific has the power to attract what you want into your life. Pull the anchor up from your 'Someday Isle' and set sail to your Specific Harbour.

Avoid: Try Use: Will

With the type of work I do I choose to outsource the mundane things so I can concentrate on the ideas that change people's lives. When outsourcing I have learned to listen for the word *"try"* if a deadline is involved. Too many times I had let people off the hook when they say to me, "We are really busy and we'll TRY to have it completed by Friday". I have now learned to politely and firmly ask the question, "Will you have it done by Friday because I need to *know for sure*." From memory, every time I have said this I have achieved the result I wanted.

The word *"will"* cements a timeline into peoples' subconscious far better than *"try"*. The word *"try"* tends to imply failure with a pressure release valve where people can say, "Well we didn't win but at least we tried". YUK!

The fact is that you really can't *try* to do anything. You either do it or you don't. Most people use the word *"try"* when they don't want to do something and don't want to offend someone by saying *"No"*. I personally would rather be upfront with people rather than let them down. How many times have you said that you would try to call in or try to phone them and you failed to do so. We subconsciously know what we mean when we say the word *"try"* and yet we continue on as though we are doing the right thing by everyone. *"Try"* has false hope for those who are counting on you. For yourself you are creating a pressure release valve on your life. When the heat is on it becomes too easy to walk away and say that you tried. We don't even realise we are doing it in the moment but our subconscious had already received its command.

Tell yourself you will follow through. You will get what you want. You will achieve your dreams and goals.

Tip for Communicating with Others

People who inspire others to greatness do so with the power of their words. Reaching your major goals will probably require the assistance of many people. When you are looking to motivate others to help you I would recommend the use of the words, *'lets, we, together'*. Instead of saying to someone, *"Go ahead, I know you can do it"*, say to them, *"Let's go, we can do this together"* and watch them come alive. Support people and you'll have an army of help. Take some time to create and add to your own personal Success and Failure Dictionary.

HOW TO DESIGN POWERFUL AFFIRMATIONS

Be Brief

If you have ever read a long winded affirmation that walks you through just about every living characteristic on earth you will probably find them as useless as they are boring.

For an affirmation to be effective it must be brief and direct. It must be something that you can remember and repeat ANYWHERE, ANYTIME. This is why simple, one word or one phrase affirmations can work so well. When it's easy to remember, it's easy to repeat - and ultimately it means it's easy for your brain to make the neural connections.

Start by choosing the quality or characteristic that you most want to develop and mix it with one of your most powerful. If you are honest and want to become bolder then make sure these two qualities are in the affirmation.

Make it Positive

It must be POSITIVE. This is a no-brainer. You wouldn't expect a good affirmation to be negative would you?

In saying this I will give you a classic example of people who use a negative affirmation and wonder why they get nowhere. People who smoke often repeat to themselves things like, "*I will quit smoking.*" "*I can give up*". Now tell me, how many people do you know who are aiming for a successful outcome and simultaneously want to "Quit" and "Give Up". The subconscious doesn't like to quit or give up. It likes to improve and grow more complete.

If you are a smoker use, "*I will maintain and improve my lungs each and every day feeling better as I do*" or "*I am growing healthy now that I feel free from that old addiction*". Take your pick ex-smokers. Each works wonders.

Get Emotional

This is the BIG ONE! All good affirmations must be as emotional as you can make them. The subconscious accepts congruent emotions that are consistent with the words far quicker than anything else. This is why *Affirmations of Emotion* are so powerful. Just repeating a feeling to yourself has tremendous impact.

The biggest mistake people make with affirmations is they sound like a boring, dying drunk. They mumble away without any vision and conviction and wonder why it doesn't work.

Just add your favourite emotional power words and use the word "*FEEL*" in your affirmation.

Gradual - belief or doubt (in the moment)

This is the only part of an affirmation that changes to suit where your beliefs currently are. When we start out towards our goals, many of us don't believe we are capable of success. If there is a hint of doubt and we try telling ourselves something like, "*I am a millionaire*" we feel like we are lying to ourselves. And instead of programming the subconscious we can actually be making matters worse. If you are a person who values honesty then lying to yourself is about as bad as it gets. Instead use gradual words until you 100% believe in yourself and then you can change it to "*I am*". Gradual words include words like, increasing, getting better, improving, becoming, growing, raising, mounting, ascending, etc.

A Wealth Affirmation

This wealth affirmation is one adapted from the infamous Émile Coué's famous affirmation that was used in hospital for the recovery of patients when they were asked to repeat, *"Every day in every way, I am getting better and better"*. I designed it for my own personal wealth at the time and it took around three weeks for it to come to fruition. It was...

WEALTH - Every day in every way I am becoming bolder, taking more action and becoming richer ... and I love it.

An important point I should mention here is that even the word WEALTH on its own has great power. The success with all affirmations depends on filling your mind with what you want and keeping your mind off what you don't want. One word alone can do this. If you are ever stuck trying to remember what your affirmation was, just remember that the keyword will do it, so long as you have the emotion to back it up.

Mirror Technique

People often ask me, "How will I know when I truly believe in myself?" I suggest they perform the mirror technique. It is a way of flushing out any doubts.

The eyes are commonly referred to as the windows to the soul. The soul is often just another word for the subconscious. By looking into the mirror and repeating your affirmations you will be able to tell if there is a hint of doubt or not. Look deep into your own eyes and repeat your affirmation. Become aware of the feelings that well up inside of your own body.

If you feel a tendency to look away from your own eyes it often can signal doubt. Give yourself a minimum of 10 attempts in order to be sure. You will find that the more you repeat your affirmation whilst looking directly into your own eyes the more power you feel inside.

The hardest thing to do in the beginning is attach the right amount of emotion whilst looking in the mirror. It feels weird, but it shows us how little we sometimes know about ourselves. If as you continue repeating your affirmation you begin to feel more comfortable with it then I would recommend continuing with the same words.

If you find it impossible to look yourself in the eye and speak with real conviction and emotion then I would make the words more gradual until your belief grows.

Learn to understand the difference between being uncomfortable and being honest with yourself. We all feel uncomfortable the first time we do something new. I still feel uncomfortable when I start with a new affirmation. It's just something we need to persist with. You are changing the way you see yourself after all.

It is without doubt one of the most powerful forms of affirmation I have ever used. With practice you will testify the same. You'll rarely witness anyone else doing this but the stories are that many great boxers, Olympians and business people use affirmations. You simply must do this. No exceptions, No excuses.

21 DAY COMMITMENT

95% of the Thoughts You Had Yesterday You Will Have Again Today

Once you have designed your own personal affirmation I want you to stick to one and one only for 21 solid days. Do not attempt to program your subconscious with wealth and love at the same time. You will dilute one in order to fulfil the other. Just stay totally 100% focused on your current affirmation until it becomes a part of you.

21 days is how long it takes to change a habit. If we only think around 5% differently each day (due to habit) then it takes at least 21 days to be 100% changed (20 days multiplied by a 5% change in thoughts per day).

At the end of the 21 days you can begin work on another affirmation. You will achieve far more in the growth of your subconscious programming by taking these qualities 21 days at a time. Be patient and good things will come so fast it will make your head spin.

Your self-talk is either going to be your best friend or your worst enemy. Listen to your *Inner Conversation* and protect yourself from the negative world events the media loves to publicise. 21 days from now your self-talk and thought patterns will begin to shape the new you.

Points to Remember on Self Talk

1. Train your *Inner Conversation* to encourage you.

2. Use questions that create positive responses.

3. Use affirmations of thought, action, feelings and words. There's more to an affirmation than just the tongue.

4. Create your own *Success and Failure Dictionary*.

5. Design affirmations that empower you - brief, positive, emotional and gradual.

6. Take a good long look in the mirror and find your greatness.

7. Make a 21 day commitment to yourself and grow.

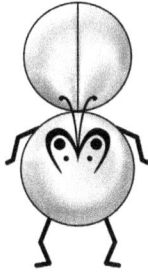

CHAPTER 9

The Life Cycle

"Success is fragile like a butterfly. We usually crush the life out of it in our efforts to possess it." - Max De Pree

LESSONS FROM THE BUTTERFLY

Change

In order for a caterpillar to become a butterfly it must endure tremendous change. I use the butterfly to remind me of the changes I must make in order to achieve my goals. If the caterpillar were capable of flying it wouldn't require changing at all. It would already be and have enough to live out its dream. For most of us we are a few changes away from being what we want to be. How adaptable are you prepared to be? Will you make the transformation that nature is asking of you in order to develop into the type of person you want to be. Every caterpillar has inside of them a butterfly.

You have inside of you everything that you need to become all you can be. Do not resist change. The old saying of, *"That's the way we've always done it"* is destined to keep you cocooned in your former self.

"People who resist change are the greatest offenders of change." -
Scott Groves.

Your journey will ask you to change and adapt. Too many people confuse this with sticking to old methods of achievement because that's what they set out to do. If a better and faster way comes along that allows you to move closer to your goal then take it. Persistence can be foolish.

Get clear on the difference between quitting and changing. To drop a method cold when it is not working and to begin pursuing a better way is smart. If you can get the same result while lying on the beach with your mobile phone in hand, licking on an ice-cream instead of getting caught up in traffic, as you pound the streets going door to door then I say well done.

Cocoon

There are many dangers in this world. As you begin pursuing your goals do what the butterfly does. Protect your environment while you grow.

We have talked about the influence of negative people. Cocooning yourself is not locking yourself away from the world. It is preparing for greatness. Cocooning yourself refers to your ability to always hold your desires, reasons and strength within. It is fine to talk about what you want to achieve. Some students of the subconscious will tell you that this can disempower you. I believe that if you keep your reasons and strength within, you will always hold the power. Reasons are the personal fuel that will give you the strength to fight your way from the cocoon of the past and give you the wings to fly.

"Stand guard at the door of your mind." - Jim Rohn

Struggle Makes Us Stronger

A butterfly's transition into flight is not an easy one. Nature's grand plan requires a butterfly to fight its way through a tiny opening it makes in the cocoon. This forces the fluid from its body into its wings where they will dry, ready for flight. If helped along by human hands when trying to escape the cocoon, the butterfly will fail to develop enough strength in its wings and never be able to fly. Although our heart goes out to the butterfly in its moment of struggle, any attempt to assist would cripple it. They develop their strength through the resistance of freeing themselves. Freedom could only come after a struggle.

There will be some struggles that we simply must fight on our own. It is these struggles that give us the strength to know that we can survive anything.

Any time you are faced with difficulties, adversity and resistance, I want you to think of the lonely butterfly, hanging from the limb of a tree all alone, fighting with every fibre of its being; and know that this is the secret to its success - and yours. Through struggle we learn to appreciate the beauty of our personal transformation and the wonder of the world that awaits us.

"We all begin crawling before we can ever fly."

Unique

Like a butterfly, you are unlike any other part of creation. When you look in the mirror remind yourself that there is no one else on this planet quite like you. Be proud of the fact that you're different. You're unique in your own special way. As much as we look up to others and admire qualities in other people, I believe you should become your own admirer. You have a combination of qualities that when compiled create a special someone. Everyone is here for a reason. We make of it what we will.

"Always remember you're unique,
just like everyone else."

Life is Short

Let me share with you a sobering story that jolted me into perspective. I gave my Mum a phone call for her birthday only to find my sister answer the phone to give me the news. My mum was in hospital on her birthday with a hiatus hernia that was attempting to burst through her belly button. She lay in pain, all alone at the hospital with her only son and only grandchild over two thousand kilometres away. Naturally we had no warning and there was little we could do given the distance.

A nurse on duty was kind enough to take a cordless phone in so I could wish her what felt like a rather empty birthday wish. Our conversation was filled with the usual chit chat of a son and mother.

It wasn't long before a nurse who needed the phone back came in and before I knew it our conversation had ended. I am embarrassed to say that I hung up the phone from her and I didn't tell her that I love her. The second I hung up the phone I realised what I didn't do.

Just a few years later, I flew home to be with Mum and spent the week with her in hospital. I got to tell her everything I wanted to tell her. Just how much I loved her. Just how grateful I was for everything she ever did for me as a kid growing up.

I was there holding her hand as she took her last breath.

My Dad's health has not been good for the best part of 35 years. We rarely had an active father-son relationship. It is only from photographs that I remember him holding us in a pool on a summer holiday in Mildura, the most northern and warmest point in Victoria, Australia.

For more than a third of a century he has doggedly fought with his health. There have been so many operations that even he has probably lost count. For a period of almost two years he was being admitted to hospital about two weeks out of four.

One particularly dark day came when he was due to go in for a life-threatening operation to remove two thirds of his pancreas that had literally turned as hard as concrete. It was life-threatening surgery. I can still remember watching him being wheeled away from our sight as we searched the right words just in case this was it.

He came through his operation and spent the next three days in intensive care. It was not a pretty sight. I can still remember looking into my fathers eyes and seeing the fight, the pain and the cry for help as he lay motionless. It's an unwritten, unspoken bond that forms between a father and son in moments such as these. A connection like no other. A resolve handed down from one generation to another. An unspoken promise from father to son to never end up like he has. I cannot to this day express in words the feelings that well up inside of me when I think about my father's life and what he has missed out on. I have sent him material that I have written, just to keep him positive in the hope that some miracle may happen.

It wasn't long ago that my sister took Dad to hospital again and completely out of character Dad plucked the courage to ask, *"How long do you reckon?"*. The doctor's response was, *"At least a year"*.

For as long as I can recall I cannot remember my father ever asking a question like this. If he did, he has never shared it with me until now.

To see a proud man like my father reduced to a forty some kilogram frame with little muscle mass and aged face is difficult. I have been brave for so long. I have tried to encourage him and motivate him in every positive and negative way that one can conceive. The one thing I wish I had done more of is love him. I am making up for this now. I have tried to be someone that he can be proud of and I know he is. How we treat those closest to us, in their moment of need says a lot about the type of person we are. When their back's are to the wall and the doctor says one year when your father wants ten, where will we be?

I'm sure anyone reading this can appreciate my excitement in finishing this book. Something I have been working on for many years. This book is important to me because I now see how it brings together the culmination of what I have learned through the experiences that my parents have brought me.

Life really is short. Never forget the things that are most important to you.

A butterfly only lives for two weeks. In the grand scheme of things, as humans, you and I are not so different. Time goes so quickly for us. One minute we are children in the arms of our father, splashing around in a pool of memories and the next time we look up we are thinking about what it might be like without them.

If butterflies could talk I am certain they would say "*I love you*" before they ever leave their cocoon.

Promise yourself that you will tell those you care about the most how you really feel about them. The one thing I have learned is that you will never say "*I love you*" to those you care about enough times. You will probably look back and always wish for one more minute. But life doesn't work like that. We are each given the right amount of time on this planet to do what we were put on here to do. Dream big dreams. Fall in love with family, friends and foe. Tell people how much they mean to you. Leave a legacy behind for others to follow. Draw strength from the hard times and be courageous enough to find the positives in all situations.

I have had many mixed feelings as I have matured watching our family go through these turbulent times together. All I see now is the courage of my father. A human spirit that has never given in. I believe it is something that we each possess. At age 58 he still talked about his dream of getting a new car and driving up to the Gold Coast where he can be with his granddaughter.

He never made it.

Dad's declining health meant he could never travel again. Whilst he managed to stretch his life out 12 more years, he never managed to fill them up. He suffered quietly and elegantly on the sidelines while the rest of the world was being experienced.

Whilst I wish my fathers life had been different because I believe he deserved better, I am grateful for the courage and the 'will to live' he showed me. That resilience allowed him to hold in his arms 4 beautiful grandchildren before he passed. But he missed out on more than he experience. It is a lesson that will stay with me for as long as I live.

Life teaches us in funny ways. Lessons present themselves right when we need them the most. Throughout this book you may have found this to be true. Answers to life's questions are not something that you can get from a book; they must come from within. With each understanding that you develop from internalising the information that this book contains, you expand your possibilities. With each reason you develop for becoming all you can be, you begin to tap an energy and determination that no force on this earth can stop you from becoming.

Now that you understand some of my reasons for doing what I love to do, I want you to go and find yours.

Live each day as though it's your last. Plan for tomorrow and live for today. No more regrets. No limits. Leave behind a legacy that others can be inspired by. Make *The Power of Subconscious Goal Setting* your own and with it you can do anything.

Significance of the Butterfly

There is an ancient story that a friend of mine told me about. Thousands of years ago it was believed that when people were faced with decisions in their lives, they could simply pick a direction and begin moving towards it with patience and faith. If it was the right decision it would not be long before a butterfly would cross their path. It is believed that if you see a butterfly it means you made a wise decision and you are on the right track.

Every time I go walking I find more and more butterflies crossing my path and I will forever remember this story. It gives me a sense of certainty that I am on the right path.

Every time you see a butterfly, I want you to think of this ancient story and remember that you are travelling in the right direction. When you stay true to yourself and your dreams you will begin to see butterflies everywhere.

Your friend

Scott Groves

Scott Groves

A Gift to You from Scott Groves

FREE for ALL
"Subconscious Goal Setters"

From the Desk of Scott:

I want to give you the entire 71 page Action Planner for FREE!

This normally only comes as part of the live seminar series but with the release of this second edition, I just want you to have it.

Simply head on over to the website.
SECRET CODE: THANKSGROVER
("I'm sure you'll find the link.")

Have a Team? Ask about Team Licensing
or you can order bulk copies direct from our website.

Think BIG! Act BOLD! Have FUN!

ScottGroves.com